Matt Qvortrup

The Brain and the Ballot Box

Matt Qvortrup

The Brain and the Ballot Box

The Politics of Social Neuroscience

DE GRUYTER

ISBN 978-3-11-161619-3 (Paperback)
ISBN 978-3-11-161691-9 (Hardcover)
ISBN 978-3-11-161650-6 (PDF)
ISBN 978-3-11-161654-4 (EPUB)
DOI https://doi.org/10.1515/9783111616506

Library of Congress Control Number: 2026948034

Bibliographic information published by the Deutsche Nationalbibliothek
The Deutsche Nationalbibliothek lists this publication in the Deutsche Nationalbibliografie; detailed bibliographic data are available on the internet at http://dnb.dnb.de.

De Gruyter and Walter de Gruyter GmbH are part of De Gruyter Brill.
www.degruyterbrill.com

Questions about General Product Safety Regulation:
productsafety@degruyterbrill.com

Cover illustration: spawns/E+/Getty Images

This book is dedicated to staff at the Beachside Rehabilitation Unit, Mona Vale Hospital

Acknowledgements

The author wishes to thank Dr Jasmine Gilchrist and Dr Karen Chia, both Mona Vale Hospital, for their expertise and for an encouraging and a stimulating environment.

 | https://doi.org/10.1515/9783111616506-202

Contents

Introduction

"I thought you were teaching political psychology, not science fiction." We were co-teaching a course at the Defence Academy in Wiltshire, and we started chatting between classes. I was a television broadcaster at the time, but I had been allowed to moonlight as a lecturer. So here I was, delivering a class on political communication to aspiring officers with varying degrees of legal knowledge. While I was at liberty to choose the topic of my lectures, pitching my course presented an unprecedented challenge.

After much contemplation, I landed on the topic of social neuroscience with an angle on criminal trials. While discussing the discovery of my interest in the topic and my approach to teaching the function of the brain in revealing the culprit of a crime, Roger glared at me quizzically after his exclamation.

"That is what my session is about. This is certainly not fiction, in fact, it has been done already." And, I continued, "One of my case studies is a criminal trial from India in which a woman was found guilty after a brain scan revealed that the lying centre of the frontal lobes were activated when she feigned innocence".

It is still early days for this political science of the brain. We cannot exactly read other people's minds, but we know enough to have a fair idea of how the political brain works.

Feeling that I had captivated my audience – Roger was a bit of a science buff – I went on. "I can also tell you which party you are likely to vote for based on fMRI scans. If you want, I can even tell you whether you prefer Coca Cola to Pepsi."

"If this can be really used in my line of work, I'd like to see a book about it. Let me know when you write it." So, Roger, if you are reading this, here it is.

And so, here we are, 10 years later, with the book. Naturally, a lot of proverbial water has passed under the equally proverbial bridges of social neuroscience since then. But, essentially, the chapters that follow are a continuation of my chat with Roger.

As I told you, to date, there have been limited attempts to analyse brain scans to gain insights into human behaviour that are relevant to the field of political science. Conversely, there have also been attempts by biologists to apply their knowledge to political subjects. My goal, above all, is to introduce this thinking to people who are sympathetic to, but unfamiliar with, the brain and how neuroscience can elucidate our knowledge of political science. The contents of this book are a continuation of the research and findings of experts in the field of *neuropolitics*, which, in turn, is part of a larger discipline called social neuroscience, all of which, in turn, answer questions that were previously left unanswered by social

 | https://doi.org/10.1515/9783111616506-001

scientists. Why do people develop an "authoritarian personality"? Why do we prefer one candidate to another? Why are liberal parties so spectacularly unsuccessful? And how might this change?

This little book is rather different from other works in the field of social neuroscience because it addresses how the ideas of political philosophy have a neurological correlation – or, in other words, a neuroscientific perspective on political philosophy. It looks at brain science through the prism of political theory, including (but not limited to) the ways in which the political psychology of Plato can be understood through fMRI and fNIRS scans (a revolutionary new technique that has hitherto not been used in political research).

All books have a gestation period. This book originated when I was a visiting professor at the Australian National University. My experience led me to author an academic book, *The Political Brain: The Emergence of Neuropolitics*, published by CEU Press, written for political neuroscientists and based on a programme I developed in 2023 during my time as a regular presenter on the BBC Radio 4 Analysis programme titled *The Democratic Brain.* In this programme, we interviewed brain scientists and political consultants and discovered, much to the surprise of the former, that the latter were already using the insights of cutting-edge neuroscience to influence customers and voters. Needless to say, this programme was rather complex for the average BBC Radio 4 listener. I am grateful to my producer, Bob Howard, for asking probing questions and for forcing me to explain concepts that may not have been entirely obvious to those without a background in neuroscience. In 2024, I was invited to give the prestigious *Philosophy Share Lecture* in Valletta, Malta.[1] My lecture, "The Democratic Brain: Body, Soul, and the Politics of the Listening", is reproduced in Chapter 8 of this book. The book also contains material I presented at the Political Theory Seminar at *LUISS* in Rome when I was an adjunct professor at that august institution in 2024. I am grateful to Professor Valentina Gentile for inviting me to present my paper and to colleagues there for their input and constructive criticism.

I am also grateful to my friend Mark Fullbrook, former Chief-of-Staff to the British Prime Minister, for helping me understand the economic and strategic implications of the new science of neuropolitics and for inviting me to present these ideas at a staff seminar for Fullbrook Strategies Limited. I am also indebted to Harry Lambert for inviting me to speak at the Neurotech conference at the James Crick Institute in London in October 2024. His deep understanding of neurolaw helped me reshape my ideas on the use of social neuroscience in legal practice. Above all, I am grateful to Stella Cavedon for research assistance and editorial support. Working with passionate and insightful young researchers is a pleasure and a blessing.

While I did study neuroscience in the long and distant past, and although I have often given talks on the topic as a political consultant and while I was working as an academic, this book was not written with the scientific community in mind as the target audience. Henceforth, I am approaching this subject as a reporter and not as the neuroscience researcher I once was. To be sure that my reporting is accurate and correct, I have relied on conversations with distinguished colleagues and experts. These include, among others, Professor Barbara Sahakian from Cambridge University, Professor Dr Darren Schreiber, Professor Skyler Cranmer, and especially Dr Liya Yu, whose book *Vulnerable Minds: The Neuropolitics of Divided Societies* prompted me to put my thoughts down on paper.[2]

As the author, my initial ambition was to write a concise book that gradually revealed that the link between politics and the brain is irrefutable. However, this approach fell short of reaching my goal. Collectively, this book consists of ideas and chapters that are in many ways disjointed but together succeed in offering the reader a circular understanding of the proof and importance of the subject I am addressing. In many ways, I am not alone in struggling to meet the call for order and progression, the kind that builds towards a singular, illuminating moment. The philosopher Ludwig Wittgenstein (1889–1951) revealed this in the preface to his posthumous masterpiece, *Philosophical Investigations* – which I take the liberty of quoting in full.

He wrote,

> My thoughts were soon crippled if I tried to force them on in any single direction against their natural inclination. And this was, of course, connected with the very nature of the investigation. For this compels us to travel over a wide field of thought criss-cross in every direction. The philosophical remarks in this book are, as it were, a number of sketches of landscapes which were made in the course of these long and involved journeys. The same or almost the same points were always being approached afresh from different directions, and new sketches made. Very many of these were badly drawn or uncharacteristic, marked by all the defects of a weak draughtsman. And when they were rejected a number of tolerable ones were left, which now had to be arranged and sometimes cut down, so that if you looked at them you could get a picture of the landscape. Thus, this book is really only an album.[3]

The Brain and the Ballot Box likewise comprises "sketches" of different "landscapes". This book reveals how brain scans can give us a whole new understanding of why we make decisions that may not appear rational – such as stance on immigration, tax and welfare.

Before we go any further, we should not only give credit to those who came before us but also explain why this discipline is a revolutionary step towards transforming the fields of political science and sociology. Some of my colleagues have written as follows:

> Neuropolitics, an emerging field to study the interplay between neuroscience and politics, investigates brain mechanisms underlying complex political information processing such as political cognition and decision-making. Compared to commonly used surveys in political science studies, brain imaging measurements are more objective, more precise and less biased measurement techniques to evaluate questions in political psychology.[4]

If you have some reservations about this statement, you are not alone. It is a bit bold to say that neuropolitics is objective. We don't yet know enough about the brain to claim that we are near to an objective analysis. And social neuroscientists are not objective in their choices of subjects. Like everyone else, they have political preferences, private agendas and pre-existing belief systems. Therefore, when a celebrity (it was the actor Colin Firth, if you were asking) asked a group of social neuroscientists to identify what "went wrong" in far-right young men's brains, the nature of his question was inherently making an assumption. The results of the study, analysed and published in the report *Political Orientations Are Correlated with Brain Structure in Young Adults*, were scientific in nature. However, given that the agenda of the study can hardly be considered objective, it seems unfair to assume that the results acquired through objective means be judged as unquestionably true. Given the biased nature of the question that prompted Colin Firth's study, the possibility that there was a vested interest in showing that conservative young men were using a particular reptilian part of their brains makes it so that even science is not immune to human partisanship (we shall come back to this later).[5]

The first to use the term "social neuroscience" in the early 1990s were careful to say that there were many ways of looking at human behaviour and spoke of "multi-level analysis".[6] Focus groups, interviews and opinion polls are all integral aspects of social neuroscience studies. Social neuroscience and neuropolitics can also complement other research by offering a level of substantiation or a rebuttal to a theory that is difficult to challenge. But that said, fMRI scans and more recently fNIRS scans, can show things that may be unwelcome for some – and certainly give us insights that others may find embarrassing.

For example, the young men in the study sponsored by the star from *The King's Speech* and *Bridget Jones' Diary* did use the *amygdala*, a part of the brain that is associated with hatred and fear, when they were thinking about politics. This part of the brain is the one that we use when we have knee-jerk reactions to things, when we don't deliberate and just act on pure instinct. There is no other interpretation of this fact. This is an "objective" truth. But, of course, it does not follow that they are therefore less intelligent than other people. We should add here that using the part of the brain that we share with rats, cats and bats is not the sole preserve of right-wing young men. People who are angry – whether on the Left or on the Right – can be driven by anger and hate, and this can spill over into their political behaviour: in how they vote, what they shout at demonstrations and much more besides this. You will shortly learn all about it.

Alice Springs, NT, Australia, April 27, 2026

Chapter 1
How the Brain Works: A Crash Course

"'Psychochemistry', yes would you believe it?" The philosophy professor looked at the audience and smirked. They laughed sycophantically – it seemed like a good idea for their grades. It was a safe bet.

I was particularly excited. As a student in the medical faculty who wanted to understand the brain biologically as well as philosophically, this field was news to me. I had to attend the philosophy lectures as part of my freshman orientation, but I did not know that there were other people who pursued this line of work. As it turned out, the professor of psychochemistry had passed away a few years earlier when his tractor overturned on his hobby farm, or something like that. But I was still able to get a copy of his book from the natural science library.

Much of what I read at the time is still valid, but the world has moved on in many ways. So, before we look at neuropolitics and all the wonderful (and spooky) stuff it can lead to, it is necessary to get the foundations right in order to understand how it all works. This is a field where there are rapid developments. When we began studying neuroscience in the late 1980s, we had a vague sense of how the brain worked and only a very imperfect ability to observe it in practice.

Let's start with the basics. The adult brain is made up of about eighty-six billion cells called neurons. They differ in size from 4 to 100 μm. They all have the same shape and function. When we think or do any other cerebral activity, whether playing the piano, debating immigration figures or joggling ping-pong balls, it is because neurons fire neurotransmitters from one end, called the axon. These enter the gap between nerve cells (called the synapse) and are received by a *dendrite* (to use a technical term) attached to another neuron.

We discovered this at the end of the nineteenth century. The starting gun was fired when some rather beautiful images of neurons were produced by the Italian scientist Camillo Golgi (1843–1926). In 1873, used silver staining to visualise what neurons looked like. However, Golgi did not think that neurons by themselves were that important. At the time, many believed that the brain was one large bundle. This, if you care to know, was called the *reticular theory*.

After this, the Spaniard Santiago Ramón y Cajal (1852–1934) entered the scene. He was a histologist (an expert in tissues, if you didn't know). By studying the brain cells of birds, he showed that these were not all connected and that they were not all bundled together. This theory became known as the neuron theory.

 | https://doi.org/10.1515/9783111616506-002

In science, as in everything else, there are real-life dramas and stories. Both Cajal and Golgi were important for the development of neuroscience. But to put it mildly, they did not see eye to eye. They disagreed on practically everything. So it was a bit awkward when they shared the Nobel Prize for Medicine in 1906. Had it not been for these two rivals, we would not be where we are today. So, which of these two scientists had it right? In the end, Cajal's theory was corroborated due in part to the invention of the electron microscope, but also to studies of traumatised brains (we shall come back to those shortly).

It is one thing to say that neurons are the key to understanding the process of thinking. It is quite another to explain why. To truly comprehend this mechanism, we need to go back to, well, psychochemistry.

So, how does it work? A bit of elementary chemistry is needed. You'll need to concentrate. Are you ready? Here we go. The nerve cells (yes, neurons) are negatively charged (with chloride atoms). When a neuron is activated, the membrane is opened, and positively charged sodium atoms enter the brain cell. This causes a chain reaction, which spreads up the body of the cell and ultimately leads to the end of the neuron. Once it gets there, so-called neurotransmitters, which are stored in small pockets (we call these vesicles), are released and find their way into the synapse (which is the gap between the nerve cells). Once out there, the neurotransmitters are received by another neuron.

The key to any brain activity is neurotransmitters, of which there are about 100. They are broadly divided into two types. On the one hand, there are so-called excitatory neurons. Excitatory neurons increase the likelihood of a message being passed on to another neuron. On the other hand, there are inhibitory neurons. Inhibitory neurons decrease the chance of this process succeeding. Excitatory neurons release neuro transmitters that encourage them to fire. One example of this is glutamate, which is associated with learning and memory, and this transmitter accounts for about 90% of all activity in the brain. It is also associated with alertness. Without going into the complex biochemistry of the matter, it is important to note that increased caffeine intake raises glutamate levels in the brain.[7] As I write this, I am drinking coffee, and it is 2 PM. That might not sound all that odd. But this drug remains in the bloodstream for a long time. Half of it will still be in the system after 6 h. So maybe this explains my sleeplessness – and, who knows, yours?

Inhibitory neurons, on the other hand, release inhibitory neurotransmitters. That is, they slow things down a bit. One example is GABA (gamma-aminobutyric acid, but you need not remember that!). It is one of the neurotransmitters that block or prevent the message from being passed along. For example, if you have an epileptic seizure – the equivalent of a thunderstorm across the brain – you can take GABA reuptake inhibitors (or GRIs) to slow things down a bit. It should perhaps also be noted that GABA plays a role in the way marijuana works. If you smoke a joint, everything will appear in slow motion because marijuana reduces the uptake of excitatory transmitters.

There are many exciting neurotransmitters, but they account for very little of the overall activity in the brain. These are often produced in specific areas of the brain. One example is oxytocin. It is produced in the hypothalamus and released by the pituitary gland. Often referred to as "the love hormone", it plays a crucial role in social bonding, trust and, indeed, love. But it also plays a crucial role in childbirth and lactation. All this we may find wonderful, motherhood and apple pie and all that. And, certainly, at the individual level, it is a good thing that we love and trust one another. But there is also a negative side to it. We may develop an obsessive love for our nation or the group to which we belong – so intense that it leads us to hate others with an equal but opposite passion. Neuroscientists have found that this ethnocentric nationalism is associated with higher levels of oxytocin.[8] For some of us, this may seem entirely negative. Still, we should not deceive ourselves. In situations of war or the presence of an outside threat of aggression, a sense of kinship with one's tribe is essential to survival.

Of course, we must proceed with caution. The researchers who studied this neurotransmitter in its more positive form were at pains to add that "oxytocin is not the molecular equivalent of love. It is just one important component of a complex neurochemical system that allows the body to adapt to highly emotive situations."[9] The same is, of course, also true of the role played by this transmitter in ethnic conflict and prejudice.

For the purposes of a book on social neuroscience and the politics of the brain, two neurotransmitters stand out. They are, respectively, serotonin and dopamine. The first one is connected with sex and sleep and, crucially for the purposes of this book, "serotonin is positively correlated with sensitivity to social factors and modulates social behaviour in a 'for-better-and-for-worse' manner".[10] Serotonin is often in the press. Sometimes it can get a bit sensational. For example, the Harvard School of Medicine wrote on its website (in a blog) that "when you feel happy and all seems right with the world, you're feeling the effects of serotonin. This hormone is responsible for boosting mood."[11] Of course, it is a bit more complicated than that, but sometimes we need to put things a bit starkly to get the message across. Not just for journalists but even for a top-ranking American university.

Dopamine is perhaps even more famous. The bestselling book *Dopamine Nation*[12] explained that it is not just pleasure that is associated with this neurotransmitter; it is also connected with motor control. For example, a reduction in dopamine levels is responsible for many of the symptoms of Parkinson's disease. More importantly, dopamine is the substance that increases in the brain during the anticipation of rewards.[13] So you get a kick (a rush of dopamine) in the synapses when you get excited by sport. That book, being American, used baseball, but in other parts of the world it might be cricket or soccer (football). But there are other aspects of dopamine that may be somewhat more worrisome for people. For example, many Class-A drugs work by affecting dopamine levels in the brain. Take the case of cocaine. It gets its effect by blocking the removal of dopamine from the synapse. This means that those who take this drug are in a state of perpetual bliss. The problem is that cocaine users become so accustomed to unnaturally high levels of dopamine that normal joy seems bland. Consequently, they lose the ability to enjoy non-chemically induced happiness. This becomes a problem when the system demands ever-higher doses of dopamine, that is to say, more cocaine.

This is not intended to turn this book into a drug-awareness course. The point here is simply to explain how it all works. And neurotransmitters are an important part of this story – and one that is easier to explain when we refer to real-life events.

Of course, all this, as you will have realised, is a bit more complicated. So let's get a bit deeper. When dealing with dopamine, it is important to know that there are two types of receptors for this neurotransmitter: D1 and D2. The functions of these receptors have been explained with admirable clarity in a recent book, as follows:

> Each receptor class has slightly different physiological properties, affinities, and localization within the brain. D1 receptors are proportionally more abundant in the prefrontal cortex, the frontal area linked to goal-directed decision-making, cognitive control, and high-level reasoning. In contrast, D2 receptors are concentrated and expressed in the striatum, the snail-shaped cluster of neurons that constitutes the largest recipient of dopaminergic nerve ends in the midbrain. The striatum computes expectations about consequences of our actions. It encodes the associations we forge between rewards and stimuli as well as between rewards and the actions we take to achieve them.[14]

What is interesting is that these are relatively rare. There are more than 80 billion nerve cells, yet only between 43,000 and 230,000 dopamine neurons.[15]

However, when dealing with social neuroscience, we do not directly get involved in the psychochemistry of the brain. Perhaps, in the distant future, this might become the case, but for now, those who use brain science to study human behaviour in society focus on parts of the brain that fire up in scans when people perform a particular activity. And, to a degree, the identification of different types of dopamine neurons suggests that we are on the way there. What is more important for the moment – and for the purposes of neuropolitics – is that certain areas of the brain can be associated with different patterns of activation, which in turn can help when we try to sell products or get people to vote for political parties. To explain exactly how, we need to shift our focus a wee bit.

A few years ago, someone criticised a blog I wrote. Normally, I do not pay much attention to such criticism. After all, there are a lot of people who get very angry about small things, and, frankly, life is short. But in this case, my critic called me an "electrophrenologist". That is a rather neat, if difficult, word. Phrenology was a discipline that is now discredited. It was invented in the nineteenth century, when researchers began to study the brain in earnest. At the time, the German medical doctor Franz Joseph Gall (1758–1828) proposed that certain parts of the brain were responsible for certain predispositions. These tendencies could be measured by the shape of the skull. So, based on bumps on the head, you could – so he argued – determine our personality. Herman Melville referred to it as a credible theory in his famous novel *Moby Dick – Or the Whale*. The Native American Queequeg's

> Head was phrenologically an excellent one. It may seem ridiculous, but it reminded me of General Washington's head, as seen in the popular busts of him. It had the same long regularly graded retreating slope from above the brows, which were likewise very projecting, like two long promontories thickly wooded on top. Queequeg was George Washington cannibalistically developed.[16]

But even among scientists – or rather, especially among them – there was widespread scepticism about this theory. When Queen Victoria had her grandchildren's crania checked, time was already running out for phrenology. More experimentally minded neuroscientists were looking at the microlevels of the brain to understand how it worked. This led, first of all, to some rather remarkable images of brain cells – or neurons, as they soon became known.

But before we get to that, we ought to mention the curious case of Phineas Gage. He was a railway worker. He was hit by a long iron pole while he was supervising an explosion. It penetrated his skull through the eye and shot up into the frontal lobes. Miraculously, Gage survived, but he was never the same. His behaviour changed overnight. Previously, he had been courteous and polite. After the accident, a physician who examined him reported that he was, "fitful, irreverent, indulging at times in the grossest profanity (which was not previously his custom), manifesting but little deference for his fellows, impatient of restraint or advice when it conflicts with his desires . . . A child in his intellectual capacity and manifestations, he has the animal passions of a strong man."[17] What the case of Gage shows us is that traits of self-restraint and social intelligence (or their lack thereof) are associated with exactly those parts of the frontal lobes that were destroyed. Gage survived because the accident affected only parts of his brain associated with cognitive functions – none of the ones that are to do, say, the heart, digestion, endocrinological secretion, etc. The Gage case is mentioned in nearly every book on neuropsychology because it proves that certain parts of the brain are activated when we engage in social behaviour.

All this was branded "localism" and was ridiculed. Still, although it was discredited during the age of phrenology, many experiments continued to show that certain areas – albeit in interaction with others – were responsible for patterns of behaviour. For example, in the 1950s, the English-born Canadian psychologist Brenda Milner carried out experiments on the patient H, who had his hippocampus removed following a botched lobotomy. The hippocampus, we need to add, is the part of the brain associated with long-term memory. There are several interesting studies that show this. I can't resist mentioning an example.

A few years ago, the father of a friend of mine was part of a study. My friend's dad is a London cab driver. But to drive a black cab – one of the iconic London taxis – you need to pass "the knowledge". That is a test – run by the London Metropolitan Police – in which you have to literally memorise all immovable objects within a six-mile radius of Charing Cross Station, literally every street, landmark and route within the city. Only those who can do this will get the certificate to drive a Hackney Carriage – as it is also called. So, with 25,000 streets, you need a pretty amazing memory to accomplish such a task. Of course, this intrigued neuroscientists. So, they selected a group of cab drivers (including my mate's dad), collected data and found that although these individuals had average IQ, their posterior hippocampus was considerably larger than average. They wrote,

> The posterior hippocampi of taxi drivers were significantly larger relative to those of control subjects. A more anterior hippocampal region was larger in control subjects than in taxi drivers. Hippocampal volume correlated with the amount of time spent as a taxi driver (positively in the posterior and negatively in the anterior hippocampus). These data are in accordance with the idea that the posterior hippocampus stores a spatial representation of the environment and can expand regionally to accommodate elaboration of this representation in people with a high dependence on navigational skills.[18]

Okay, I admit, this is not the most poetic prose. But you get the idea: the hippocampus is related to memory, and this was what Milner initially found when she studied H. As a result of his accident, he had no short-term memory. What was crucial about this was that the complete lack of this part of the brain showed that localism still plays a role – though only in connection with other parts of the brain. This was an important finding, one that essentially laid the foundation for the current paradigm of neuroscience.[19]

So, focusing on parts of the brain, as Millner did – albeit in interaction with other parts – allows us to predict beliefs and behaviours. This is a novel, revolutionary development – though one that has yet to be fully appreciated and utilised in political thinking. But we need to be mindful of the nuances, for the rightful fear of being accused of sensationalism.

So, let's get back to the fundamentals. The brain is not simply divided into areas that are responsible for specific tasks or thoughts. Several areas have multiple functions. It would be an oversimplification to say that a centre such as the amygdala (an evolutionarily old part of the midbrain) is the fight and flight centre. At the same time, this part of the brain is associated with these feelings, actions and emotions. So, as a shorthand – and as a necessary – simplification, activation of this centre is a meaningful finding. We will see that activation of this part of the brain is more pronounced among populist voters, those whose motivation for engaging in politics is fear and hate. We shall return to this in the next chapter.

But to be scientifically accurate, as a study pointed out, we should talk about connectivity playing a larger role in some areas than in others:

> The human brain is characterized by structural and functional connectivity within and between regions. Structural connectivity refers to the anatomical organization of the brain by means of fibre tracts. Recent advances in magnetic resonance imaging (MRI) and image processing provide various means to quantify structural connectivity in a non-invasive way using short-range local measures and/or long-range tract tracing procedures, called diffusion tractography. Functional connectivity refers to statistical dependence between time series of electro-physiological activity and (de)oxygenated blood levels in distinct regions of the brain.[20]

If you want to put a scientist's name to this paradigm, it would be that of the Russian neuroscientist Alexander Luria (1902–1977). He was the author of the much-cited – and rather well written – book *The Working Brain.*[21] This study presented the now-prevailing theory that different areas are specialised to carry out particular roles; however, these specialised areas are not sufficient on their own to produce a function (e.g. language). For thoughts to occur, "different brain modules act in an interdependent manner in much the same way that a complete symphony is dependent upon the coordinated performance of different sections of an orchestra".[22]

So brain science has moved on since the localism of Gall (see above). But it is still the case that certain functions are mainly associated with particular parts of the brain, and that we can see this in fMRI scans. Overall, then, the Functional Systems Model states that the unit of receiving and analysing information is associated with different areas of the cerebrum, such as the occipital lobe (vision), the temporal lobe (inter alia, auditory functions) and the parietal lobe (tactile sensation), and that these are transmitted to the frontal lobes (cognitive and executive functions) for analysis and assessment. For Luria, then, it was clear that the prefrontal lobes performed a superior role as "a superstructure above all other parts of the cerebral cortex . . ., a far more universal function of general regulation of behaviour".[23]

When I first studied these things, we had limited ways of looking into the brain. We were limited to the electroencephalogram (EEG), a test that measures the electrical activity of the brain. These could, at best, show different graphs of where there was activity in the brain when it was stimulated. That is not unimportant, and a lot can be learned from this relatively inexpensive technique. However, EEG tests do not give us a clear picture of what is really going on inside our brains.

Back then, it must have been in 1989, one of the young professors was excitedly telling us about CAT scans. A CAT scan is a medical imaging technique that uses X-rays and computer programmes to generate detailed images of the inside of the body. These were impressive, but X-rays can be dangerous.

The following year, a Japanese researcher called Seiji Ogawa made a groundbreaking discovery: you can measure the levels of blood flowing to different parts of the brain. Since nerve cells need oxygen, and oxygen is carried in the bloodstream, monitoring blood flow can offer insight into brain activity. Given that blood is magnetic because it contains iron, it is possible for us to detect changes in blood oxygen levels using an MRI. By converting these neural changes into computer-generated images, scientists can visualise which areas of the brain are most active. For example, when you are trying to memorise a particular route to take (if you are one of the aforementioned taxi-drivers), we can see that more blood flows to the hippocampus, which is used for navigation and memory. This technique is called functional magnetic resonance imaging, or functional MRI (or fMRI for short).

To say that Seiji Ogawa's invention caused a revolution in neuroscience is an understatement. Certainly, this book – and the entire study of social neuroscience – would not exist but for fMRI. Still (and I shall tell you more about this later) there are limitations to this technique. For starters, it is very expensive. A one-hour session costs $1,000 per person. Moreover, and of greater concern for researchers, you must lie perfectly still when you are shown photos or films. Conversely, politics is an activity practised in social gatherings. A rally, for instance, is a political act performed by a group. Given that fMRI cannot be conducted live on multiple subjects, how are we to apply Seiji Ogawa's findings to social emotions in group politicking?

One way of doing this is to use fNIRS (functional near-infrared spectroscopy). Like fMRI, fNIRS measures brain activity by detecting changes in blood oxygenation levels in the brain. But instead of measuring magnetism, it uses near-infrared light to see changes in the light's properties as it passes through the skull and returns to a computer. This technique cannot probe, and generally, can only record activities in the outer layers of the brain. It also does not provide the same high-resolution images. The advantage of fNIRS is that it is effective for studying multiple people in mobilised social groups. There are pros and cons to all techniques; however, when combined, they give us a rather good understanding of what happens in our brains when we think, when we make purchases and when we shout obscenities at politicians we dislike.

Armed with this new information, let's get to work. We have a lot more to learn, but we'll pick it up as we go.

Chapter 2
Candidate Selection and the Brain

“Did you stay up for Liz Truss?” My friend – a Labour candidate for the 2024 UK general election, was positively beaming. The shortest ever serving prime minister in British history had been ejected from Parliament in the Conservative Party’s biggest defeat, and Ms. Truss had not endeared herself to voters (or anyone else) by not giving the customary concession speech. She’d been a bit of a sore loser, violating the age-old tradition of “loser’s consent”, which goes alongside the fundamental principle that a democracy is a system under which governments lose elections because politicians are held accountable by their constituents.

I had stayed up late. I was in New York, and the result ticked in at 11:48 PM – twelve minutes to seven in her Norfolk constituency.

Truss was defending a majority of a whopping 26,000 votes – and now she’d lost. Sure, the margin was a mere 600 votes. But a defeat is a defeat.

“Serves her bloody right”, said my friend. He was not exactly magnanimous in victory. He had failed to win the election himself, and now he consoled himself by taking comfort in Truss’s defeat. It was, he admitted, “a classic case of *schadenfreude*”.

This, of course, is a favourite German word among the British and Americans. Lisa – of *The Simpsons* – explained to her hapless father that it was, “a German term for ‘shameful joy’, – taking pleasure in the suffering of others”.

To which Homer Simpson replied, “Oh, come on Lisa. I’m just glad to see him fall flat on his butt!”

“Oh, come on” I responded. “Give her a break.”

My Labour friend would have none of it.

“I guess, that is just the difference between the way your brain and my brain works”, he said combated.

I was about to launch into an extensive scientific delineation, but something told me that he was not in the mood to hear about the neocortex, the amygdala, and all that.

Perhaps you see it differently? Perhaps you, too, stayed up to see Liz Truss fail? Maybe you even remember the “Michael Portillo Moment” – when back in 1997 the then poster boy of the Tory right lost his seat?

If my friend had been in the mood to listen, I would have explained that *schadenfreude* could be located in the brain with rather more precision than you would perhaps have thought.[24]

 | https://doi.org/10.1515/9783111616506-003

Hidehiko Takahashi and his colleagues in Japan – a country where people generally have greater respect for a person higher up the pecking order[25] – ran an experiment that yielded particularly interesting results.

Firstly, they asked a group of people to read information about privileged people. Then, they were told that those people had suffered misfortune. When they were first presented with the information, they felt envy, and there was a strong activation of the anterior cingulate cortex (I shall come back to this later in Chapter 8, but it is the part of the brain associated with unfairness). What happened next was more pertinent to our own (or at least mine) thoughts regarding Ms. Truss. For when the participants in the experiment were told that the privileged group had suffered bad luck, there was activation not only in the ACC but also in the ventral striatum – the part of the brain that is, among other things, associated with pleasure.

The ventral striatum activates during experiences of schadenfreude, and this brain activity closely matches self-reported levels of pleasure. A statistical correlation supports this connection, as noted in the endnote.[26]

Basically, the two go together; the self-reported feeling of glee when someone falls "flat on their butt" (metaphorically speaking) is matched by activation in the ventral striatum.

So far, so good, but our Japanese friends were sceptical – or maybe just methodical? Maybe there was something special about Japan that made people prone to *schadenfreude*? As you may know, the Japanese have a common saying that translates to "The misery of others tastes like honey." And, if you have watched Japanese television shows like *Takeshi's Castle*, where normal people endure (sometimes painful) humiliation in a slapstick way, you might be tempted to think that we (or the Japanese, at least) just like to see other people suffer?

To find out, Hidehiko Takahashi and his colleagues conducted the same experiment with people of low status. And, perhaps, to their surprise (they don't say), the ventral striatum was not activated when these people were not envied.

So, *schadenfreude* is something we feel especially towards people who do better than us. And these feelings are more common in people who vote for parties on the Left than among those who vote for parties on the Right.

I don't want to go too much into that right now. Most of all, because I want to tell you more about it later. You can skip ahead now and read Chapter 9 if you are impatient. But if you are patient, you will bear with me. Or you can read the box about patience below:

The Social Neuroscience of Patience

Some people just can't wait. They want instant gratification like in a "I Want It Now/Oompa-Loompa from 'Willy Wonka and The Chocolate Factory'". If you just want to have your chocolate bar (or any other craving) you will likely activate the ortomedial prefrontal cortex. This is the part of the brain just behind the eyes, and it is what one neuroscientist has called "the strongest candidate for linking food and other types of reward to hedonic experience".[27] But if you are a more patient person, you will activate the medial prefrontal cortex (mPFC) – the area just above. It is the part of the brain that integrates information and regulates emotion, motivation and social behaviour. So, in a sense, this is the patience part. But it is not that simple. Nothing in the brain is. When we are patient – when we are able to resist temptation – it has something to do with the regulation of the neurotransmitter serotonin between the mPFC and the OFC. Serotonin is the chemical messenger that affects your mood, emotions and digestion. Exactly how this works is somewhat open to speculation. Experiments on mice – which do not have these parts of the brain – show that higher serotonin levels lead to patience.[28] When people who are suffering from depression take serotonin, it often reduces their libido. However – and this can get a bit complicated – there are two different forms of serotonin. One of them, the so-called 5-HT, is an inhibitor, and it blocks uptake and is associated with the feeling of craving. However, there is another form of serotonin, called 5-HT(2C), which increases erections in men and sex drive more generally.[29] This is not the subject of this book, really. I admit this. But I think you will find it interesting. Don't you?

The fact that we can predict the ideology of a person is partly to do with feelings of envy – and *schadenfreude*. It also has to do with other parts of the brain. Conservatives, as a general rule, are more cautious than Liberal voters. This means that they activate a part of the brain called the dorsolateral prefrontal cortex. It is the part at the top and to the side, and it is normally associated with being a bit on guard, a bit hesitant and a bit sceptical. Basically, a bit well "conservative".

You might conclude that conservative people are not risk-takers, that they think carefully before they act. But that is not really the case. This is because we have two areas of the brain associated with caution. The dlPFC is associated with scepticism, whereas the ventrolateral prefrontal cortex, located just below, is responsible for self-control, the "think-before-you-act" kind of things.[30]

Being a political person, of course, also has something to do with our sense of self. I might say that it is a part of who I am to be "a conservative" or "a liberal," and that is part of my identity. If so, it is not surprising that the ventromedial prefrontal cortex – the part of the brain in the middle next to the central sulcus – the gorge that divides the two hemispheres – is associated with what we call the "sense of self".[31]

Once again, it is a little bit more complicated in practice. Particular segments of the brain do get activated when people watch political videos; however, there is more to it than just that. Certain components of the brain react differently to the stimuli. In an experiment, some American researchers played small film clips for voters and found that there were marked similarities between those who identified as conservatives and those who identified as liberals:

> After watching each video [about Trump's idea of a Border-Wall to Mexico], participants rated the extent to which the video made them more or less likely to support the relevant policy on a five-point scale. The responses were recorded such that higher ratings denote attitude change toward the conservative position (e.g., more likely to support the construction of a border wall) while lower ratings denote attitude change toward the liberal position (e.g., less likely to support the construction of a border wall).[32]

I am sure you will think that this is not social neuroscience, just simple social psychology and a bit of arithmetic. Quite so; however, what the researchers also found that the participants had different levels and patterns of brain activation in their dorsomedial prefrontal cortex and ventral striatum when they were shown the videos.

Not to be outdone, or perhaps just to prove a point, Oriel FeldmanHall and her colleagues at *Brown University* carried out a similar study. They encoded words typically associated with conservative, right-wing views and others commonly linked to the political left. What they found was that similar words triggered similar patterns of brain activity in both right-leaning and liberal-case participants.[33]

The name of this phenomenon is neural synchrony. When you look at the activation of the dorsomedial prefrontal cortex, the electrical signals that go into the computer differ between liberals and conservatives. These different "spike-patterns" expose the ideological sentiments of an individual, effectively placing them in one of two categories: liberal or conservative.

Okay, this is a bit complicated, so read this slow. First, they looked at the brain sequence patterns of the liberal and conservative case subjects and took an average of the individual graphs to make the "liberal state change sequence" and the "conservative state change sequence". They noticed that there was a higher frequency of spikes with smaller amplitude in the left-voter brain, and fewer spikes but with greater amplitude in the right-voter brain.

Using these patterns, we can almost see eyeball ideology. Of course, it is not that simple, and sometimes, in the real world, we need AI and all sorts of computer technology to separate the "reds" from the "blues" – but you get my drift. And, perhaps, who am I to say, you already feel that you, too, can spot differences in the graph.

These examples of neural synchrony take place in the dorso medial prefrontal cortex. This part of the brain deals with the sense of self, which incorporates social impressions and what psychologists and philosophers call *Theory of Mind*, meaning the ability to understand others. The Czech politician and playwright Václav Havel once wrote that

> Ideology is a [. . .] way of relating to the world. It offers human beings the illusion of an identity, of dignity, and of morality while making it easier for them to part with them. It enables people to deceive their conscience and conceal their true position and their inglorious modus vivendi, both from the world and from themselves.

I have to admit that his phrasing is not exactly elegant, and I had to read it several times over. He might not have known the neuroscience behind his statement, but he basically got it right.[34] The way he explains it pretty much fits the research – only he reached it by a different route.

Ideologies are the way we see the world, the colouring we give it, so it stands to reason that this should show up in our brains in different ways. For someone who is conservative, as well as for someone who is liberal, having a belief system is a way of putting things into perspective and a way of turning a chaotic world into bite-sized pieces. Some might say that ideologies are simplified accounts of the world. This is true. In fact, this is the point. To navigate through the world, we need to simplify the complicated.

This, when you think about it, also makes sense when we think of our evolution as a species. Paralysis by analysis is not a particularly helpful thing if you are face-to-face with a grizzly bear or a lion. Nor, for that matter, is it helpful when you are faced with a high-stakes moral decision. Therefore, when we are driven by an ideology – by a sense of self and a theory of mind – it is through this that we make decisions.

I should add that neural synchrony is but one way of separating Conservatives from Liberals. Different people use different techniques, and like in the famous Japanese film *Rashomon*, the truth can be seen from different angles. If you haven't seen it, the film follows a murder trial in which each of the witnesses tells the same story but in slightly different ways, and it allows the viewer to appreciate that the world, and the things we see, are always coloured by perspective. It is not that everything is, as the famous saying goes, "in the eye of the beholder". We can talk objectively about the world, but we need to acknowledge subtle differences. There is not one perspective that is the right one – not even that of neuroscience. This is just one way of looking at things.

But all this is a bit theoretical. It is about belief systems: the things that make us tick. But you might be sceptical and say that people often vote for reasons that differ from their real values.

You may be an obsessive who thinks about politics all the time. In fact, you probably are, as you are reading this book. But many people pay more attention to football, fashion or scrolling on TikTok, Instagram, X or whatever platform is currently in vogue. The factors that influence a final voting decision often depend on elements unrelated to policy. These include a candidate's image, background, slogans, overall vibe or other aspects entirely disconnected from political ideology.

The advantage of using social neuroscience is that we can now say with certainty whether we are driven by ideology or whether other factors play a role. These conclusions can be drawn by scanning brains during presidential campaigns.

Political campaigns have the goal of changing people's minds. They are about getting people to vote and, sometimes, to vote for things that may not benefit them. The reality of political agendas, regardless of ethics, is winning. Politicians are in the business of winning elections, and all is (regarded) fair in love and war, as we say.

All this does not mean that all voters are susceptible to these largely unpolitical factors. However, elections are often decided by a narrow margin. Gaining the favour of voters who are not ideologically aligned with you as a candidate can mean the difference between victory and defeat. For political consultants and hired guns who are in the business of persuading voters, these tactics are crucial. For you as a political consumer – a voter – knowledge is power. Knowing that politicians will be utilising information regarding your brain's response to word patterns and your emotional susceptibility will make you think critically regarding your own voting outcome.

So, where does this lead us? Well, basically, we can use brain scans to find out which candidate we find most attractive. This is, of course, interesting if you make a living out of getting politicians elected to office. But that is a niche business. Being a voter is not. Knowing that political consultants may (increasingly) be using these techniques is useful to know when you make up your mind about whom to vote for. Would you vote for a candidate who is using these techniques to convince you? Should you? I leave that question to you.

Chapter 3
The Social Neuroscience of Failure

Why Liberals Lose and How the Left Could Win Again

"Socialism . . . is based on a lively sense of wrongs crying out for redress"
G.D.H. Cole[35]

Once, the Left would always win. When the rich got too rich and the poor too destitute, the pendulum of politics would swing to the left. No longer. The tendency is the same everywhere. Liberals lose. Consistently. You could start anywhere. Like Kansas. A native of the landlocked Sunflower State lamentfully mourned,

> Not long ago, Kansas would have responded to the current situation by making the bastards pay . . . When business screwed the farmers and the workmen . . . when it ripped off shareholders and casually tossed thousands out of work – you could be damned sure about what would follow. Not these days. Out here the gravity of discontent pulls in one direction only: to the right, to the right, and further to the right.[36]

These words, though written at the beginning of the century, have not ceased to be true. The political divide between those who believe in a larger role for the state and those who do not has given way to the culture wars. The Right has swung to the right, comfortable in its slightly newer skin. The Left is trying to find its feet, with mostly spectacular lack of success.

Once, it was so easy for Liberals. Tax the rich. Appeal to class consciousness. But that is no longer the case. The parties of the Left are anxious to appear financially prudent, so they have abandoned the old rhetoric. And they lose all the same.

Maybe that is the nature of politics. Time moves on. Politics does too. But social neuroscience has another answer. One that explains the recent successes of the Right – and the concomitant failures of the Left.

I have already spoken about the Conservative brain, how those on the centre-right activate the dorsolateral prefrontal cortex and how those further to the right have heightened activation of the right amygdala when prompted by images and other stimuli.

But the liberal brain is an altogether different story.

It's the story of envy, empathy, and equality – and a bit of argumentative fact-checking. I write this not on the basis of any surveys, still less on the basis of psychometric tests of the sort you fill out for higher managerial jobs. My focus on the three "Es" is based purely on scans of people who happen to vote for left-wing or liberal parties.

 | https://doi.org/10.1515/9783111616506-004

Equality

Not long after the 2015 General Parliamentary Election, I was invited to speak to an audience of former Labour Members of Parliament. It was a distinguished crowd, and a dejected one. They believed they would win, but they lost again.

Launching in with fMRI scans and graphs would probably alienate them. Instead, I decided to play a little game with the audience. It was the Ultimatum Game, a favourite among HR specialists. The type of "game" you have to play if you are being recruited for a cut-throat job in the financial industry.

It goes like this. Two players are given $100 to share – but only if they can agree. Player One takes $70 for himself and leaves the remaining $30 for Player Two. If Player Two rejects the deal, neither gets anything. If she accepts the deal, she gets something, although she may consider it unfair. When played in job recruitment, most players simply accept the money, even if the division is 90:10. After all, you are better off than you were before.

Not so in the case of the former politicians.

"I'd rather have nothing at all," said a female ex-MP. She seemed upset, almost offended by what she had just heard.

"But", I asked (perhaps) rhetorically, "you would be better off with $30. Wouldn't you? So, why reject it?"

She didn't hesitate: "Because, it's a dick move. It's not fair. Somewhat disgusting to insist that it is more beneficial just to shut up and take 'something'". Everyone nodded and murmured. "Hmmm, disgusting?", I inquired. I had them exactly where I wanted them: "Well, then, I have something to tell you", and carried on with my slides – one of them is below. For they all acted to form. For there is a difference in activation of the brains of Liberals and Conservatives when they play the Ultimatum Game.[37]

People who reject the unfair offers have activation of the anterior cingulate cortex and the insula – the very parts that characterise the "liberal" brain – though also the dorsolateral prefrontal cortex, which is normally associated with more conservative thinking.

Why is all this significant? Broadly speaking, and leaving out the inevitable caveats, we know that the anterior cingulate cortex, or ACC (as it is called in the business), is involved in processing fairness, unfairness and social exclusion. So it stands to reason that this part is activated when you receive an unfair offer.

To reiterate, it's the fairness part of the frontal cortex. Not, mind you, that it acts alone. All parts of brain interact with other parts, as we have already established previously. The ACC – especially the middle (or "medial") part thereof – gets activated when we try to restrain ourselves – and is connected to other parts of the brain, such as the amygdala and the insula. But the kind of anger an unfair offer elicits in a "liberal" brain is different from the one of someone with right-wing views. On other occasions, and in other people the ACC may put a damper on the blind rage that characterises amygdala responses in more conservative voters.

In the case of "unfair" offers, people of the Left often have activations of the insula. This, you will remember, is the part of the brain associated with empathy. But it is also a part of the brain associated with disgust. So, when someone of the Left – like our ex-MPs – receives an offer, they can find it "disgusting". Perhaps it was not that surprising that the one-time Labour MPs used this word to describe an unfair offer in the Ultimatum Game.

At this stage, one of the former politicians raised an objection.

"Why, Professor, is it that the conservative part of the brain gets activated?" He dragged out the title "Pro-feeeesorrr" with a slight hint of disdain. In England, as opposed to the Continent – and even America – there is a kind of inverse snob effect, and being a "professor" is often code for "who-do-you-think-you-are"?

I do not recall my exact response, but it was something along these lines:

> We all have to show restraint. Out on the savanna millions of years ago, our ancestors needed to be cautious. If not, they would have been eaten. Evolution favoured those who had a sensitive dorsolateral prefrontal cortex. Whether we are conservative or liberal (or Labour) the neural circuits which are our thoughts always double check if a decision is risky, and for that reason, you will see activation of the dlPFC (as it is called for short).
>
> You see – if we simplify a bit – this is the cost-benefit part of the brain.[38] It is only natural that a Labour person checks the benefits of a decision, especially one that is associated with money. We all have this capacity. People on the left think about money too. It's just not their overriding concern.

But not all people react in this way.

When I relayed the story to a former Conservative cabinet minister, she described the rejection of offers as "childish".[39]

"For goodness sake, they are better off. So, why?" For her it was, as she put it, "just a cost-benefit analysis". But she, too, admitted that "the choice could become so pathetically small, that you just want the other person to stuff it".

She too activated her "fairness" and "disgust" centres, even if her overriding concern was founded on a cost-benefit analysis. In other words, typical conservative voters and politicians, such as our Tory ex-minister, showed less activation in the anterior cingulate cortex and the insula when playing the Ultimatum Game. Though she too could experience a sense of "disgust" at "unfairness", it was to a lesser extent. Social neuroscience is not categorical. It is not black-and-white but rather shades of grey, much like the colour of the brain itself, as it happens.

It is these nuances that you need to understand if you want to utilise the insights of neuropolitics to your own advantage. And this is what the Left has consistently failed to do.

"I am intensely relaxed about people getting filthy rich as long as they pay their taxes", said the New Labour Minister Peter Mandelson in a speech to Silicon Valley executives.[40] (And, yes, it he was also sacked as UK ambassador to Washington for his association with Jeffrey Epstein, but that is another story.)

That this Oxford-educated politician, who was sacked for his association with the filthy rich, had such views – and was a member of the Labour Party, is one thing. But it does not follow that all Labour voters have the same view. Indeed, far from it.

Before we go any further, let's have the usual caveats – and then move on to why these may not be quite so necessary for social neuroscientists.

So, here we go. It is, of course, always contentious to talk about politics. But you will probably agree that Tony Blair (and other politicians of the Left) went to great lengths to woo the capitalist class, to show that they were "responsible" and the like. There are good reasons for this. Politicians must be competent managers of the economy to be entrusted with power. And the Labour Party has often been accused of being a spendthrift. The fact that most crises of capitalism have occurred after long periods of rule by the Right in America, such as the Wall Street Crash in 1929 and the financial crisis in 2008, has not had the effect of making liberal parties more trustworthy for the monied class. So those on the Left are locked in a constant battle to appear fiscally prudent, as the line goes. But there is a problem with this strategy. For in their eagerness to win, these parties have forgotten the voters' – their voters' – concerns. And these revolve around fairness. For the average Labour voter, equality – and fairness – are important, and being "filthy rich" just doesn't cut it.

For Labour – and similar parties such as the Social Democrats in Germany, the Socialists in France and Democrats in the United States – to win again, they must appeal to the parts of the brain that get activated when their voters are presented with matters of equality, empathy and envy.

When using social neuroscience techniques, we still need few caveats. But as the next couple of sections will show, we actually have a fairly good idea of what makes the average leftie tick – we can read their minds, and – while we may not like what we see – it gives us a literally graphic idea and an objective understanding of the liberal mind.

Empathy

You need to be a bit cautious when you talk about the brain in relation to the sections that are associated with political ideology. The way we have mapped the brain is relatively arbitrary. So when we have a part of the brain such as the insula, you need to know that not all parts of this is associated with, in this case, empathy.

You will remember when I told you about disgust above and how some Liberal voters were "disgusted" by someone taking the lion's share of the money. This activated the insula, too. And to make matters even more complicated, we have also seen that Conservatives are generally driven by feelings of disapproval. These feelings also reside in the insula, but just the front – or anterior – part of it.[41]

To summarise, when we see activation of the liberal brain, it is not in the whole structure but merely in the left insula and in the so-called posterior – or hind end of it.[42]

Maybe this is what happened in France in 1975 during a presidential debate?

"*Vous n'avez pas le monopole du cœur*", meaning "you do not have a monopoly of the heart", was the famous line in a presidential debate used by the Centre-Right candidate Valéry Giscard d'Estaing against his socialist opponent, François Mitterrand. It is credited with winning him the election that year.

The Conservative candidate appealed, if not to the heart, then at least to the anterior insula, the deep-seated part of the cortex that is activated when we feel empathy towards others. Whatever your politics may be, it is safe to say that those on the Left are primarily concerned with social welfare. Leftists are labelled "socialists" for a reason. By appealing to this instinct, Giscard d'Estaing won re-election. And 7 years later, he lost it when Mitterrand more successfully appealed to the heart, a.k.a. the posterior insula and the so-called temporoparietal junction.[43]

Some Conservatives will undoubtedly say – and with some justification – that they too have a social conscience. Of course they do. We all do. We would not have survived as a species if we did not have the ability to experience empathy. Back in the day, in what we now call East Africa, where we first evolved, those who possessed a gene that prompted them to look after other members of their community had a higher likelihood of survival than those who lacked genetic factors contributing to empathetic sentiments.

All things being equal, those on the Left are more susceptible to emotional appeals by politicians: to empathy arguments. In this regard, there is solid evidence. Some German researchers scanned the brains of voters who had made donations to political parties. They discovered that those who had given money to parties on the Left had higher activation of the insular cortex than those who had not, and who were therefore less motivated to make donations by emotional appeals.[44]

Of course, this is a rather indirect connection. Giving money to a party that champions social equality is not the same as showing empathy. Especially in Germany, where the conservative party, the Christian Democratic Union, has always emphasised that it takes its Christian roots seriously. Indeed, in Bavaria, the sister party is called the Christian Social Union. Therefore, it is entirely possible that these findings do not prove anything at all about the reasons why some would give money to one party rather than another. What we are interested in is not tax-deductible donations to a political party that we may sympathise with – or to a candidate we want to curry favour with.

This type of research might excite academic seminars. But they are not really of much use to those who want to win elections, and still less so to those who are struggling to find out why they always lose.

For instance, if you are a leading member of the German Social Democratic Party – which has gone from winning nearly 50% in the polls around the turn of the century to a paltry 17% (and often less) – you might be reassured to know that there are still people who will give you money. However, you are probably more interested in knowing what makes people tick and what makes you attractive in the minds of those who really matter, namely the voters.

It is this part that excites people on the Left – and intrigues people on the Right – when I give presentations. For it is not just when wealthy individuals give money to left-wing parties that the posterior insula is activated in scans.

In fact, there is evidence to show that people who vote for parties with a more socialist or liberal outlook activate the posterior left insula when presented with video clips and statements while in a brain scanner.

In the study *"Red brain, blue brain: evaluative processes differ in Democrats and Republicans" (Figure 1)*, some colleagues of mine scanned the brains of 82 Americans (a large number in comparison with the smallish numbers normally involved) to observe differences in the brain function of conservatives and liberals while engaging in risk-taking tasks during brain imaging. They found that "Democrats showed significantly greater activity in the left Insula". Conversely, Republican voters' brains showed greater activation of the amygdala. If you look at the image above, you will see what this looks like in an fMRI scan. The little blue dot on the top image is the left posterior insula. In the fMRI, the area lights

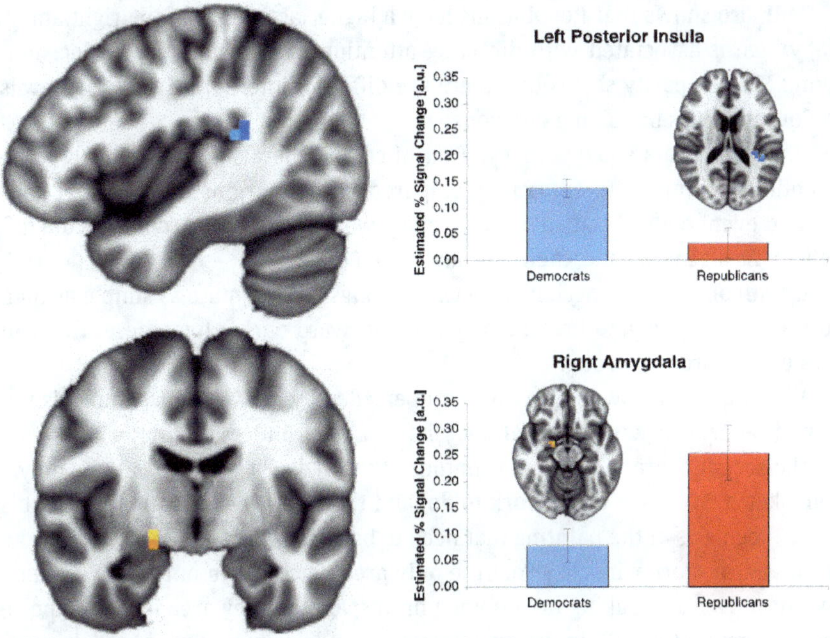

Volume	x	y	z	Side	Area	t	p
Dem>Rep							
384	-36	-40	18	Left	Insula	3.153	0.002
Rep>Dem							
448	20	-6	-10	Right	Amygdala	3.774	<0.001

Figure 1: The empathetic brain.
Source: Schreiber, D., et al. (2013). Red brain, blue brain: Evaluative processes differ in Democrats and Republicans. *PLoS one*, *8*(2), e52970.

up when blood flows to this region of the brain. The left posterior insula is responsible for internal emotional experiences, and it signals the connection between interoceptive changes that influence decision-making outcomes. In the brains of Liberals, the left posterior insula lights up when they are shown images of people in need or people they would feel sorry for.

If you now look at the little bars to the right of the scans, you will note that there is a measurable difference in empathy levels between Democrats and Republicans. This shows that Democrats are nearly three times more likely to experience feelings associated with empathy than Republicans, according to this study.

fMRI also shows that Republicans have a higher activation of the right amygdala, which is associated with directing attention to external cues in decision-making. This disparity shows that there are different internal drives for Liberals and Conservatives in making decisions.

What these data show is that in 98% of cases, Liberals are more likely to be susceptible to appeals to empathy. Compared to the margins of error that pollsters and even medical statisticians normally work with, these are minuscule differences. As a general rule, then, we can spot a Leftist.

As with all things, especially in science, things are not quite as simple as that. Natural sciences live and breathe by putting forward daring hypotheses that can be tested and proven wrong.

What we know now is likely to be superseded by new evidence, but it is unlikely to be proven wrong. We already have a good understanding of the social (and the socialist) brain. The main contour of the artwork is there, but it is only a rough sketch. We have more work to do, and there might – if I can still use this picture – be parts of the painting that need to be redrawn.

The left posterior insula is not the only area pertinent to our understanding of political decision-making in Left-wing brains; another key area is the temporoparietal junction (or TPJ). Interestingly, this region hasn't received as much attention in political neuroscience research. It's like a part of the picture we haven't fully painted. Because the TPJ's role in political orientation hasn't been studied as extensively, we can't say with certainty whether its activation is a unique feature of liberal brains. But before diving deeper into this, let me briefly explain what the TPJ does. TPJ is a region of the brain involved in distinguishing oneself from others, which plays a crucial role in empathy, perspective-taking and social understanding.

This is what psychologists call "mentalising" or, should I say, the art of understanding the thoughts, feelings or perspective of others.[45] If we assume that people on the Left are more sensitive to other people's suffering than those on the Right, then perhaps, as some of my colleagues have speculated, a "stronger TPJ activation in the leftist group compared with the rightist group may be linked to differences in their perspective on the social world".[46]

Figure 2 below shows the area that was activated among the Liberals when these individuals witnessed another person falling victim to pain. The TPJ is the leftmost part of the brain, the victor to the west, if you will. It is the part of the brain that we can see turn darker when liberal subjects are experiencing empathy.

You will also note that other areas of the brain are activated. You may be asking yourselves, "Why am I not talking about these other parts?"

Essentially, because many parts of the brain are activated' and they are not all equally relevant to what we seek to discover. The fact that the hind part of the brain is activated during this study, for example, is because we are perceiving an external stimulus.

The bottom (or inferior) occipital lobe is the part of the brain that processes visual information, and it therefore comes as no surprise that this should also turn a darker shade on brain scans throughout the study. The people in the brain scanner are obviously watching people in pain, so, naturally, this part of the brain is activated. But whereas the TPJ is actively involved in "mentalising", the occipital lobe is merely enabling this process. Therefore, it is relevant for us to analyse the TPJ. However, this brings some uncertainty, as the TPJ overlaps with another key feature associated with the liberal brain: sensitivity to fairness.

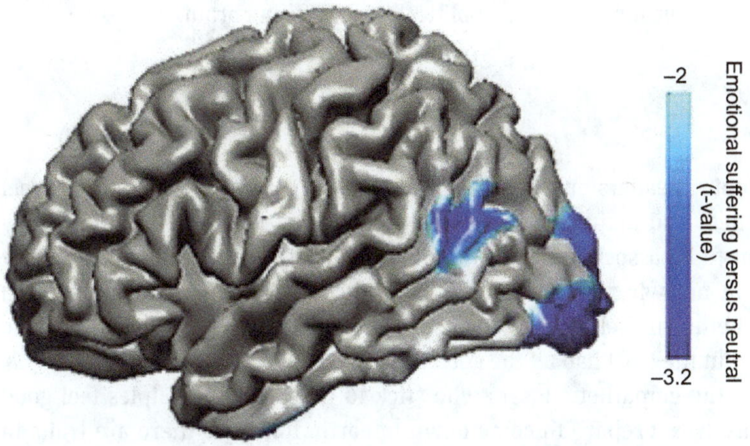

Figure 2: Another empathetic brain.
Source: Zebarjadi, N., et al. (2023). Ideological values are parametrically associated with empathy neural response to vicarious suffering. *Social Cognitive and Affective Neuroscience, 18*(1), nsad029.

What is perhaps most remarkable about social neuroscience is that it travels well and that it is not dependent upon culture in the way that many historical and sociological theories are.

Whereas political scientists talk about "path-dependency" and unique differences between political cultures and so forth, the unique benefit of our findings in political neuroscience is that they show us that we are all universally remarkably alike when it comes to observable brain functions. Not only that, but Leftists in both America and Europe show the same pattern of observable brain behaviour and perception as do people from South Korea.

The activation of the TPJ is an example. When asked questions about a scenario where an executive of a company breaks the rules to achieve a result, those of a more Left-leaning persuasion were quick to pass negative judgement by intuitively detecting violations of fairness (i.e. moral engagement). On the other hand, Conservatives were more likely to accept this decision, probably because accepting authority is a common characteristic among those who vote for and support the parties of the Right.[47]

You might ask whether the TPJ is also activated during the Ultimatum Game, which I told you about before? Good point, if you thought of that. Yes, there are studies showing that those who are particularly upset about getting an unfair share in the Ultimatum Game activate the right temporoparietal junction.[48] But again, this is a different kind of empathy. Comparing others' gains with your own is less about feeling pain than about fairness. What is essential here is that both are part of the typical make-up of a politically Left-leaning brain.

Envy

Up to this point, readers on the Liberal side of the political spectrum might feel smug. Fairness and empathy are socially desirable attributes. Hardly anybody would want to be associated with unfairness or apathy. But feeling good about yourself will not win you elections. It is a bit like the American singer Tom Lehrer – a Leftist himself – who sang about how the Right "may have won all the battles . . . [but the Left] had all the good songs".[49]

At least the empathetic losers who stick to their lofty principles feel good about themselves. Prepare to come down to earth, folks, for there are traits in Leftist brains that are less desirable. People on the Left are envious, or so statisticians tell us.[50] More often than not, the people I speak to on the Left dismiss this by saying that they don't believe the statistics, that the sample size might be wrong, and so on. That the same people then go on to cite other surveys, well, that is politics. We see what we want to see.

But when I go on to show them that the parts of the brain that are associated with envy tend to get more activated in people of the Left persuasion, they pause for thought. Perhaps it's just that fMRIs have a certain authority that we do not normally extend to social science?

In any case, the questioning does not stop there. A typical response goes like this:

"What exactly do you mean by 'envy'?"

We don't need to be fancy about it. The most common definition is the one used by the Ancient Greek philosopher Aristotle, who defined "envy" as being angry at "those who have what we ought to have".[51]

The Christian writer Tertullian, who lived in 155–220 CE, listed envy as one of the seven deadly sins, and the Catholic Church still holds this view. People on the political Right often say that their opponents are suffering from envy. Leftists can hardly be blamed for feeling insulted by their rivals' accusation of committing a deadly sin.

But it is a charge that has always worked. Perhaps the allegation has always been levelled against the Left. Even in ancient Greece, it was used against radicals, it seems.[52] That is why Aristotle used it as an example in his book on rhetoric. Maybe one of Margaret Thatcher's speech writers had read the Macedonian sage when she used the accusation of "envy" to have a dig at the Labour Party. It was in 1974, and she had just been elected as leader of the Conservative Party, when she (or one of the staff) penned an article in which she stated, "I reject vehemently the *politics of envy*, the incitement of people to regard all success as if it were something discreditable."[53]

The Left took the bait, exactly as intended by the then newly installed Conservative Party leader. But wait a minute, you might say, "Didn't Thatcher play the envy card to win votes?" And, you may further wonder, "Why would she do so, if this would alienate part of the electorate?"

The answer is that she was appealing to Conservative voters. She was doing what people in the business call "solidifying the base" – basically, winning the favour of the party faithful, the ones you need to appeal in order to win. And "her" voters typically are not too bothered by envy.

But that is different for Labour voters – or Social Democrats in Germany. Like it or not (and Leftists are likely to do the latter), Liberals are, biologically speaking, envious. What Margaret Thatcher and Aristotle were talking about was – predominately – money. You are envious because someone else has more than you.

And this shows up in the brain. Earning less dosh is associated with a signal in the ventral striatum.[54] This part of the brain, I might need to remind you, is part of the basal ganglia, part of the reward-processing system. Envy is a mental reaction and short-term feeling of dissatisfaction caused by someone else's possessions, their good luck and all the things we don't have. Envy is when you feel that you have less than others, which makes you less happy. At the chemical level, happiness is – broadly speaking – a dopamine reaction. Envy reduces your levels of dopamine.

At this point, we should be asking how envy can be identified in neuroscience, and what this has to do with the politics of the Left and the Right?

These are important questions, and I will get to them shortly. Before doing so, let's take a step back to look at dopamine. Dopamine is released in the part of the midbrain called the ventral tegmental area, and it travels to the ventral striatum. As envy increases, dopamine decreases and we become increasingly unhappy. When people in the brain scanners are exposed to situations where they might feel envy, we bear witness to a stark difference between Liberals and Conservatives. Those who lean to the right have no marked difference in dopamine levels when compared with those who lean to the left.

In the 1990s, it was discovered that some animals imitate others. This might not seem like the discovery of the century, but when scientists scanned the brains of macaques – a small, approximately 60-cm-tall species of monkey – they found something altogether more interesting. Their brains were seemingly in sync.

When one monkey reached for a fruit, certain parts of the brain got activated, typically those associated with movement of the limbs. But interestingly, when a monkey watched another monkey reach for the fruit, the same parts of the brain were activated, even if the second monkey didn't move at all. So, the brain of the second monkey mirrored the first one, hence "mirror neurons".[55]

Interestingly, these findings are equally applicable to humans. When someone expresses envy, we have mirror neurons that kick in.[56]

Envy, we can say, is a social phenomenon. It gets triggered in some people (typically those on the Left) if other people in a group say they have been given a raw deal, are disadvantaged and suffer hardship. When the brains of people who feel envy are scanned, we see mirror neurons in the parietal lobe and the premotor cortex get activated; the corpus striatum, the part of the brain responsible for assessment and motivation.[57]

It is not entirely clear why the premotor cortex is activated (it is at the top of the brain and is associated with planning and executing movements). However, it is understandable that the parietal lobe would be involved. This part of the brain (on the top, towards the back) is responsible for processing sensory information and helps you assess your surroundings.

Yes, all this is interesting, but the discussion here is about neuropolitics and why some people feel envy while others do not.

How the Left Can Win Again

Margaret Thatcher knew something about social neuroscience despite it not existing at the time. When she spoke about the politics of envy, she knew she wouldn't win over people from the Left. She rather spoke the language of "her" voters to make sure they would vote for "their" party. For her voters were Conservatives who were "relaxed" about envy.

The difference with the Left today is remarkable. Today, parties on the Left seem to go out of their way not to follow the same tactic and not to appeal to "their" natural constituency.

They want to appear as rational managers, not as rabble rousers. So, when people in deprived areas who used to vote for the Labour Party or for the Democrats in the United States feel left behind and are envious the rich and of the elite, they are described as "a basket of deplorables" by Hillary Clinton.

The starting point for any vendor is to find out what it is the customers want and how to provide it to them. As more and more companies are using different forms of neuromarketing to sell their wares, political parties, too, would benefit from marketing strategy – or rather said, social neuroscience.

And here we come back to the three Es – the story of envy, empathy and equality – and a bit of argumentative fact-checking. The latter is currently the only one that is receiving some attention. For we know that statements that are factually incorrect are jarring with Leftists' brains, as they tend to activate the anterior cingulate cortex – the fact-checking part of the brain.[58]

Let's be realistic. You don't win elections by pointing out that the other side is selective or, should we say, economical with the truth. You win by appealing to the things that people actually care about.

If the Left wants to win, they have to appeal to the perceived fairness of some people getting rich at the expense of others. The Left needs to appeal to the anterior insula cortex for empathy, and it needs to regain those mirror neurons that govern envy. At the moment, the far-right has a near monopoly of anger. This is directed at an allegedly self-serving "elite" whom the voters of the working classes see as enjoying the spoils. The reason the Left is losing is that it has vacated the position as the guardians and custodians of envy and unfairness to the populist far-right fringe of politics. The Liberals were successful in the past because they had a near monopoly of the heart (the left posterior insula cortex) – and envy (the parietal cortex).

Credible economic, defence and environmental policies do not really matter to electors – those who are potential customers in the socialist shop. Policy papers do not drive votes.

For them, the poetry of elections goes through the neuropolitics of emotions. Each campaign will need to look at prominent topics. No strategy fits all, but to be successful and to win again, as they used to, the Left must embrace the three Es: empathy, equality and perhaps above all, envy.

Chapter 4
Would I Lie to You?

If you are of a certain age – or just a movie buff – you might have watched Steven Spielberg's *Minority Report.* It is a fast-paced sci-fi thriller with Tom Cruise and Max von Sydow. In the film, instantaneous brain scans make it possible to detect whether people have committed a criminal act. Supremely entertaining, but a bit far out, you might think. But no, not completely. Pioneering papers – many of which are cited below – are able to literally "read" our mind to determine whether you are a criminal.

Overall, the studies of the brain and political behaviour are about reading our minds. And in this area, some rather impressive strides have been made. What is the extent of our ability to read other people's minds for clues as to their politics? What do we know? In the history of philosophy, the great thinkers talked about our "ideas". In the words of the English empirical philosopher John Locke, the idea "stands for whatsoever is the Object of the Understanding, when a man thinks".[59] For him – as well as the philosophers who came after him – these were private.

In folklore, it has long been recognised that while we cannot speak publicly, at least we could have our thoughts to ourselves. *Die Gedanken sind frei* is a famous German folksong originally from the thirteenth century. In the English-speaking world, it was brought to a wider audience by the folksinger Pete Seeger, who sang,

> My thoughts give me power
> No scholar can map them
> No hunter can trap them[60]

Well, the authors of the tune and the liberal American troubadour lived and worked before the emergence of fMRI or fNIRS.

They would have been astonished. For another aspect of this is neuroscience's ability to – as it were – read our inner thoughts. Or, quite literally, to see what we picture in our minds.

Enter the actor Steve Martin. Not, mind you, because the famous, silver-haired American comedian himself got involved in social neuroscience. To those who read the abstract of the study, it wasn't apparent at first what Mr. Martin had to do with it. The neuroscientist Jack Gallant and colleagues from the University of California, Berkeley, who carried out the experiment, reported,

 | https://doi.org/10.1515/9783111616506-005

> We recorded BOLD [it stands for Blood Oxygen level-dependent) signals in the occipitotemporal area visual cortex of the human subjects who watched natural movies and fit the model separately to individual voxtels. Visualization of the fit of the models reveals how early visual areas represent the information in movies. To demonstrate the power of the approach, we also constructed a Baysian decoder by combining estimated encoding models with a naturally sampled movie prior. The decoder provides remarkable reconstructions of the viewed movies. These results demonstrate that dynamic brain activity measured under naturalistic conditions can be decoded using current fMRI technology.[61]

So, why am I mentioning Steve Martin? Because he featured in the "natural movies". Three subjects (not a large sample, admittedly) were shown short video clips of the actor while their brains were scanned. The activity in the occipital part of the brain (which deals with vision) was then electronically transmitted to a computer, which used the information to come up with an image of the actor, albeit a blurred one. In addition to the film clip with the comedian, the respondents were also shown a video clip of elephants roaming in the wild. These signals were also transmitted to the computer, which generated tolerable representations of the animals in the wild. Literally, the researchers were able to make representations of the mind's inner eye.

The papers reported the findings with a bit of hype, which was probably a bit over the top. The *Daily Mail*, not normally a source for serious writing on neuroscience, reported that a "brain scanner 'reads' people's dreams – accurately enough to see what they are dreaming about".[62] This is somewhat overegging the proverbial pudding; the findings don't need to be hyped and are indicative of how far we have come.

Once again, what does this mean in practice? Quite a lot. And one way in which such findings could prove useful is in police detection and the courts. In fact, there are some indications that brain scans may – in the long run – replace lie detectors. This, at least, is what Barbara Sahakian, a professor of neuropsychology at the University of Cambridge, believes. She cited pioneering work by Dr Giorgio Ganis, a neuroscience specialist at Plymouth University,[63] and Daniel Langleben, a pioneer of fMRI scanning now at the University of Pennsylvania.[64]

When Daniel Langleben first conducted studies to detect dishonesty using an fMRI scanner, he used a model that was only about 77% accurate at spotting a lie, not a significant improvement over a polygraph. When a private company adopted the model, they were able to increase the accuracy to about 89%.

A study conducted by Giorgio Ganis, in which study subjects were asked about their birth dates, yielded a 100% accuracy.[65] Given that this study utilised autobiographical material rather than artificial material, we may conclude that the scanner can detect lying extremely accurately when subjects are asked inherently personal questions.[66]

Admittedly, we are a long way from widely utilising fMRI scans to conclude whether a person is guilty of a crime. Detecting whether someone is lying about their date of birth is certainly simpler than detecting the culprit of a crime. Well, once again, prepare to be surprised.

Neurotechnology of this kind has been monetised by a company called No Lie MRI. The company, quite openly, has sought to develop fMRI scans to further the development of a new generation of polygraphs.

What they have effectively done is to put the defendants into the scanner to see if they tell the truth. Some believe that this use of neuroscience has the potential to change the legal system.[67] However, this approach has been criticised. For example, Pardo and Patterson have suggested that our approach is too reductionist.[68] Yet, these criticisms, at the more philosophical level, have to be set against more pragmatic and partial studies that show that we can detect and even forecast criminal behaviour based on brain scans. Moreover, the difficulties that may exist with the technology are not a sufficient reason for criticising the approach more fundamentally. In the mid-1970s, the American Psychological Association officially concluded: "psychologists are not competent to make such judgments".[69]

Thankfully, this is no longer the case. Psychology is now used in most criminal cases. Since the 1993 US Supreme Court case *Daubert v. Merrell Dow Pharmaceuticals, Inc.*, the United States has allowed the use of psychological profiles. And before you ask, they have even expanded this to include neuropsychology. The latter happened when they refined this case in subsequent circuit court and Supreme Court decisions, in particular, the 1999 *Kumho Tire v. Carmichael Supreme Court* decision.[70]

So, why not also use fMRI scans? Some people in America have reservations. I will get back to that shortly.

But this is not the case in India, where neurolaw has been used in real criminal trials. Let's take the case of Sharma. She had gone to Delhi to meet with her lover, but her fiancée, Bharati, found out. He was not too happy, to put it mildly. But he agreed to meet Sharma at a McDonald's. When he went to the bathroom, she allegedly poisoned him. He fell and died. She denied having done anything wrong.

Judge Shalini Phansalkar-Joshi declared her guilty. Yes, she admitted that the 23-year-old university student did not fit the mould of a murderer; nevertheless, in June 2008, she sentenced her to life in prison. Why? Because Sharma's electroencephalogram left no doubt: the brain scan revealed "experiential knowledge". It proved that she had to be the killer.[71] Ever since then, the Directorate of Forensic Science in Mumbai has been running what they call Brain Electrical Oscillation Signature (BEOS) profiling. However, the researchers who carried out the studies had a rather prosaic view of the whole thing, one that seemed just a little bit too mechanical, asserting "we consider the brain as a computer, where information is stored and can be retrieved".[72]

In fairness, the Indian Supreme Court has subsequently ruled that the evidence gained from computers cannot stand alone.[73]

Outside India, some are sceptical. "It's alarming", Owen Jones, a professor of law and biology at Vanderbilt University stated. Professor Jones continues, "admitting brain-based evidence that hasn't been rigorously tested creates a false sense of objectivity—and a real risk of injustice".[74] His view is shared by judges across the United States. Thus, in America, findings based on fMRI scans were ruled inadmissible by the courts.[75] Needless to say there are ethical concerns. For example, "the possibility of predicting dangerousness via neurobiological markers raises issues concerned with potential violations of specific offenders' individual rights and civil liberties. These issues include the potential discrimination and stigmatization of offenders based on their "neurobiological profile", procedural and constitutional rights violations (e.g. violation of the privilege against self-incrimination) and criminal policy matters (e.g. the dividing line between criminal responsibility and social dangerousness). Coppola also writes that, "these might be overcome".[76] Further, should we not use all knowledge to get a just outcome of a criminal trial?

Should there be barriers to the truth in matters that concern violations of our personal security and even life? A strong case could certainly be made for the view, expressed by Glenn and Raine, that if neurobiological markers can reliably boost the accuracy of criminal behaviour predictions, "it could be viewed as ethically questionable not to use such knowledge".[77]

Researchers Sahakian and Gottwald concluded that "the evidence is encouraging and advancement of [neuro]science will certainly lead to the development of more reliable and accurate . . . techniques".[78]

You may have your own view. Perhaps, it may be related to your personal political views. But, while this discussion is for further study, suffice it to say that the prospect of predicting criminal behaviour is no longer pure science fiction.

But how does it work?

Old-fashioned lie-detectors focused on spotting a porky. So, which part of the brain gets activated when we tell fibs? To put it in slightly simplified – though still accurate – terms, lying is associated with both the anterior cingulate gyrus (at the bottom of the central *sulcus* that separates the two brain hemispheres) and the ventro-lateral prefrontal cortex. The latter is interesting, as this part of the brain (on the upper part of the brain to the side) is associated with inhibition and risk averseness. The former is interesting too, as the ACC is associated with motivation, decision-making and cost-benefit calculation. So, when we lie – which, to be honest (sic!), we all do to varying degrees – we use a combination of risk averseness (we are afraid of being caught) and the weighing up of the cost-benefit of telling a fib.[79]

What all of this amounts to is more than neuroanatomy. What these results show is that our thoughts are no longer private.

Liberae sunt nostrae cogitationes ("Free are our thoughts"), wrote Cicero in *Pro Milone*, one of his most famous speeches. As a defence lawyer (but perhaps not later as a politician), Cicero would have been concerned that prosecutors in India would have used fMRI scans to determine whether defendants were telling the truth. However, as a clever politician and debater, he would surely have found weak spots in the argument. The study that showed we can detect lies in the brain with greater accuracy than polygraphs was, in fact, funded by the aforementioned No Lie MRI.[80] And that is no lie!

There is, however, no reason to believe that this peer-reviewed article was biased or based on flawed evidence. The most likely conclusion Cicero would have drawn, had he been honest to himself, would probably have been *Liberae non sunt nostrae cogitationes*, meaning "thoughts are not free".

The aim of this chapter was merely to provide a tour d'horizon of the state of neuroscience art. Based on this necessarily brief overview, we can go on to look at how these insights can be used in the realm of politics.

Ethics and Social Neuroscience

"I assume", wrote the philosopher Thomas Nagel, "that a scan of Hampshire's brain at the time would have revealed a heightened activity in the ventromedial prefrontal cortex".[81] Who was Hampshire, you are probably asking yourself. His full name – with title – was Sir Stuart Newton Hampshire. He was an Oxford don, who had worked as an intelligence officer in France during the Second World War. And this is the reason Professor Nagel wrote about him. After the D-Day landings, a French collaborator was brought in, and Hampshire had to interview him. The man said he would reveal secrets if Hampshire promised him that he would not be executed. He had information that would potentially save dozens, perhaps even hundreds, of Allied soldiers. But Hampshire knew that we could not guarantee that the man would be spared. Indeed, one of his commanding officers had told the young Englishman that the collaborator would be shot whatever he said. So, Hampshire told him, "he could not give such a guarantee".[82] For Hampshire was an adherent of the philosophy of the great thinker Immanuel Kant, who took the view that we should not lie. For this German philosopher, it is the thought that counts, not the consequences. People who take this view are called *deontologists* by professional philosophers. Those who believe in "the greatest happiness for the greatest number of people" are called *utilitarians*. Okay, enough of the philosophy lecture. So why is this relevant? Because social neuroscientists have found that those who believe in the sanctity of moral rules activate the ventromedial prefrontal cortex. Other people would have thought differently from Hampshire. Many of us would have had less principles. Perhaps most of us – who knows? – would have thought that it was okay to tell a porky in order to save lives.

People interested in these matters often use the example of the runaway train, also known as the trolley problem. The scenario is as follows: a train is hurtling towards five children. If it continues, the children will die. However, if a large man on a bridge is pushed down onto the railway, the children will be saved, and the obese man will die.

There are, of course, any number of things wrong with this story. It was dreamt up in the 1960s by the philosopher Philippa Foot.[83] Why she had to fat shame the man on the bridge is a bit unclear. But the essence of the story is simple; the death of one person (overweight or not) is preferable to the death of five children – if you are a utilitarian, that is. When people like Stuart Hampshire are under the brain scanner, they will activate the ventromedial prefrontal cortex. However, people who have damaged this part of the brain will opt for the utilitarian choice or, as a research article put it, "patients with missing or damaged VMPFC consistently chose utilitarian responses to dilemmas that typically elicit deontological responses".[84] This is not to say, of course, that you have to be brain damaged to be utilitarian. In fact, other research suggests that people who are utilitarians are often those who deliberate and weigh up different consequences, whereas those who are deontologists are driven by emotions. Three researchers writing in *Nature* were "able to show that brain regions often associated with deliberate reasoning (i.e., the dorsolateral prefrontal cortex (DLPFC)) had greater activation when participants responded to dilemmas that often yield a utilitarian response, while brain region associated with emotions (i.e., ventromedial prefrontal cortex (VMPFC)) were more active during dilemmas that typically elicited deontological judgments".[85]

What is perhaps interesting is that people who have more conservative leanings tend to activate the dorsolateral prefrontal cortex – that is, they think in a more utilitarian way. It is not always like that, but certainly, there is a tendency in this direction.

Philosophers like to put people in boxes, but what social neuroscience shows is that we are both utilitarian *and* deontological. Most of us are emotional and deliberating; we use both the ventromedial prefrontal cortex (emotions and principles) and the dorsolateral prefrontal cortex (the region associated with weighing up consequences). This rather puts philosophical reasoning into perspective and adds a new dimension to it.

Chapter 5
The Neuropolitics of the Other

A nation, so a rueful European saying,
is a group of persons united by a common
error about their ancestry and a common dislike
of their neighbours[86]
Karl W. Deutsch

Dean was from Kirkcaldy, Scotland. He was a bodybuilder and a Scottish patriot. He was running a gym in Aberdeen, where I was working out, and, upon hearing my accent, he was eager to tell me that he was not English (he said the word with a grimace of contempt!) and then he went on to tell me the story of the Saltire, the Scottish flag with the St Andrew's flag.

"You see, the Scottish saw the smoke of two cannonballs form a cross in the sky, and at that moment William Wallace brought forward the troops and defeated the English." Certainly, the Scottish nobleman defeated the English king at the Battle of Stirling Bridge. But the first use of this weapon in Europe was during the Hundred Years' War between 1337 and 1453. I did not feel inclined to tell him this, nor to inform him that St Andrew was crucified on a diagonal cross. But that is not the point. The question that I pondered then (and now) is why people are so inclined to group together and form a nation.

Others have thought about this, of course. The American fiction writer Ursula Le Guin once defined nationalism as "hate of one's own country". Perhaps not the most elegant turn of phrase but an accurate one all the same.[87]

Finding a scapegoat is a tried-and-tested trick among politicians. And there are many politicians who are more guilty of succumbing to this than this otherwise tolerant and principled British politician. Nevertheless, it was used by Theresa May. Inspired by a book by a former editor of *The Spectator*, Theresa May made a distinction between "Anywheres" and "Somewheres".[88] In an unusual act of pandering to the darker elements of the "nasty party" (a phrase used a decade and a half before her), the Conservative leader drew attention to "us" and "them" and played on the ever existing fear of the "other".

In political science – and in political consulting – this is known as negative partisanship.[89] And it is increasingly used in elections. And the fact that these antics seem to work electorally begs the question: why? There are sociological reasons why such tactics may work: relative deprivation and other theories come to mind.[90] The question before us in this book is whether there is a neuropolitical or social neuroscience explanation for the apparent efficacy of these tactics.

 | https://doi.org/10.1515/9783111616506-006

The research to date shows clear indications that these strategies are effective because they appeal to some of the basest – and arguably oldest – parts of our brains. A couple of studies deserve to be singled out to give a sense of the state-of-the-art research.

My colleague Elizabeth Phelps and her colleagues carried out an Implicit Association Test (IAT), which is a psychological test where you are asked a number of questions that measure your unconscious bias towards other (typically vulnerable) groups, with the results then contrasted (or "triangulated") with findings from fMRI scans.

What Phelps was interested in was whether it was possible to measure implicit racism in the activation of the amygdala, a "subcortical structure known to play a role in emotional learning and evaluation".[91] And it was discovered that when "White American subjects observed faces of unfamiliar Black and White males . . . The strength of amygdala activation to Black-versus-White faces was correlated with two indirect (unconscious) measures of race evaluation (Implicit Association Test [IAT] and potentiated startle)".[92]

That there is a correlation between our unconscious racism and the faces of other racial groups is depressing, but there might be a silver-lining. The researchers also found that this correlation was only applied when faced with an unknown person's face. When participants were shown images of well-known faces (e.g. Black celebrities), there was no correlation; thus, "these patterns were not obtained when the stimulus faces belonged to familiar and positively regarded Black and White individuals".

Whether this provides any comfort, I leave up to you. When analysing the findings from a social neuroscience perspective, we can infer that these "suggest that amygdala and behavioural responses to Black-versus-White faces in White subjects reflects cultural evaluations of social groups modified by individual experience".[93]

We can then deduce that feelings associated with "the other" are positively correlated with certain brain areas, or ROIs ("Regions of Interest").

These findings chime with earlier research that shows – or at the very least indicates – that far-right extremism is associated with neural activity in the amygdala.[94]

So, given that the amygdala is the part of the brain responsible for fight and flight, could this be the key to understanding the appeal of far-right rhetoric? And, indeed, might the activation of this part of the limbic system, more generally, explain the importance of targeting of "the other"?

To answer all of this, we need to acknowledge that biology is not deterministic but conditional. That is, certain people have a particular disposition, and others do not.[95] Whether genetically based or a result of social factors, what we need to identify are the conditionals; the factors that prompt certain individuals to be susceptible to hate speech.

One possibility is that our actions – and the brain activity associated with them – may have a genetic basis. In fact, there is some interesting research that points in that direction. This suggests that individuals with certain genetic predispositions are more likely to respond in specific ways when those genes are activated by external factors.[96]

Other research, however, suggests that socio-economic factors can prompt what has been referred to as motivated social cognition.[97]

How does this work? Any sociological or political-science explanation must be open to the potentially beneficial effects of creating a sense of belonging as a mechanism for achieving greater cohesion. Hence, we can hypothesise that to have an ideology of "us" and "them" – or of "anywhere" and "somewhere" – is sociologically beneficial because it "brings people together, giving them an edge over those who lack the social glue".[98]

In line with this conclusion, research by John Jost and colleagues is particularly relevant in presenting supporting findings. They believe that some people have a psychological need to reduce uncertainty and threat, and this is activated when they encounter simplistic solutions based on anger.[99]

So, could it be that those who live in red states, or in the deprived areas of Britain that were termed the "red wall seats", where the Labour Party used to reign supreme, are especially susceptible to this rhetoric? Is it the case that people from these areas, having limited exposure to globalisation, and henceforth to people of a different ethnicity or background, are more likely to display these traits?

We have not conducted and published a relevant study in Britain; however, a study of Chinese and American research subjects displays some rather interesting findings.

In an article with the telling title "Do you feel my pain?", Xiaojing Xu and colleagues showed that when Chinese and Caucasian research subjects were shown film clips of, respectively, compatriots and Caucasians, they only exhibited a response in the anterior cingulate cortex and insula (two areas associated with empathy) when pain was inflicted on people of their own ethnicity.[100] On the other hand, the pain of strangers did not make an impact on their emotional state.[101] Perhaps, our brains are hard-wired to hate, and there is nothing we can do about it? Maybe it is just one of those sad facts of life, like the fact that I will never date the actress Salma Hayek (she has gone for a much richer man!), or that the *Toronto Maple Leafs* (my favourite NHL team) will never win the Stanley Cup – except, much more serious and tragic?

It seemed like it. When Zuo and Han carried out an experiment where Caucasians and Chinese subjects watched videos of people in pain, they reported,

> Using functional magnetic resonance imaging we demonstrate that, whereas painful stimulations applied to racial in-group faces induced increased activations in the ACC and inferior frontal/insula cortex in both Caucasians and Chinese, the empathic neural response in the ACC decreased significantly when participants viewed faces of other races.[102]

In simpler terms, what is being conveyed is that the empathy parts of the brain get activated when "your own" people are in pain, but not when those of another group suffer.

However, all the subjects who had been tested in this environment were from the countryside or from areas that had little contact with foreigners. And we know from various accounts that biases towards "the other" are often associated with an unfamiliarity of individuals who differ from us in race, political persuasion and/or sexual orientation.

One way to find out whether exposure to a multicultural population would reduce bias and increase empathy is to scan the brains of people who have recently moved from a suburban mono-ethnic society to an urban one. Researchers from the *Queensland Brain Institute* recruited people from China, who had first arrived in Australia between the past 6 months and 5 years. This is how they described their experiment:

> During fMRI, participants observed videos of own-race/other-race individuals, as well as own-group/other-group individuals, receiving painful or non-painful touch. The typical racial bias in neural responses to observed pain was evident, whereby activation in the anterior cingulate cortex (ACC) was greater for pain in own-race compared to other-race people.[103]

So far, so sad. But when they looked at people who had lived in Australia for a long time, they found something else: something altogether different and much more positive:

> [For] activation in the anterior cingulate to pain in other races increased significantly with the level of contact participants reported with people of the other race. Importantly, this correlation did not depend on the closeness of contact or personal relationships, but simply on the overall level of experience with people of the other race in their every-day environment.[104]

Again, not the clearest of language – they were writing in a scientific journal, after all. But the message is clear. If you live with other people and if you learn through personal interaction to see those different from yourself as your community, then you will experience empathy in their regard. They went on to say, "racial bias in neural responses to others' pain, as a neural marker of empathy, therefore changes with experience in new immigrants at least within 5 years of arrival in the new society and, crucially, depends on the level of contact with people of the other race in every-day life contexts".

So the more contact the Chinese have with Caucasians, the more they activate the ACC. We are not hardwired to be racists. When we have contact with people of other races, creeds, etc., we feel empathy towards them.

Nevertheless, and this is important, it's not really practical for people to just live together. And we don't have the patience to wait 5 years for a significant part of the population to develop empathy towards superficially dissimilar communities. Yes, it is, of course, a positive that the Chinese immigrants to Australia have become less racist over time. But it is difficult to see how this insight – welcome though it is – can be turned into a public policy. Sure, knowing that we are not innately racist is helpful. It is a starting point.

Getting people to live in the same areas might be a strategy, but it takes time. Besides, immigrants are often poorer and cannot afford to live in more affluent areas. So what else can we do? Basically, we become more empathetic when we are exposed to others who are unlike ourselves. This isn't a new discovery; in fact, René Descartes reached the same conclusion when he wrote "it is well to know something about the manners of different peoples, in order to form a sounder judgement of our own, and not to think everything contrary to our own ways absurd and irrational, as people usually do when they have never seen anything else".[105]

What the philosopher knew from experience is something that we can now more or less directly see in fMRI scans.

Riots and Neuropolitics

We are all the products of 6 million years or so of human evolution. All humans have a brain. It is important that we keep this in mind when we use neuroscience to understand social phenomena. Neuropolitics is – and should be – a means of understanding and humanising those whom we view as our opponents. It is important to keep this in mind when we analyse political phenomena that relate to one side of politics, such as uprisings by far-right groups.

These groups, whether in Germany in the 1930s or in America on January 6, 2021, are often driven by the politics of us versus them. Through this mentality, we are led to dehumanise members of these right-wing movements. We know this from several studies using neuropolitical approaches.[106]

So this is not something we can see only in the ubiquitous culture wars of the middle half of the twenty-first century. It has been on display in the uprisings and riots that have taken place since the beginning of civilisation.

Way back in ancient Rome, the historian (and one-time politician) Sallust – or Gaius Sallustius Crispus (86–35 BCE) – penned his book *Bellum Catilinae* – usually translated as the *War Against Catiline*.

His was a chronicle about an attempt to overthrow the Roman republic – and an attempt to explain the underlying logic of insurrection based on the rebellion by Catiline, a sore loser who would not acknowledge his defeat in an election. There can be little doubt that Sallust's book provides an explanation that rhymes with similar rebellions in the present, such as in Brazil in 2023 and, before that, in the United States in 2021.

What makes the Roman story so compelling and relevant in the light of the insurrections in Washington, D.C., and Brasília is that Catiline explicitly appealed to the "left behind" and claimed to side with the people against a corrupt elite. For example, he promised simple solutions, such as debt relief. Incidentally, Bolsonaro promised the same policy during the election in 2022.[107]

Like the "Trump of the Tropics", as the defeated Brazilian politician was called,[108] Catiline promised that all would be resolved if people followed him: "use me as your commander".

The parallels with history seem almost too uncanny to be spelt out. But Sallust is interesting not merely because he described a pattern that seems to repeat itself, but above all because he described the conditions that prevent democracies from falling apart, and – more important still – because this explains the mindset that leads to insurrections.

Why Do Men Rebel? was a study from the early 1970s in which Ted R. Gurr used the nongender neutral language of the time to explain uprisings as a result of relative deprivation.[109] It used to be what my academic colleagues call a paradigmatic book. In English, this means it created a trend and the framework for discussions among sociologists studying the phenomenon. It was a good book. It still is! Gurr was a serious and judicious scholar. He stressed – based on facts and figures – that "there is not much support for the view that political violence is primarily the recourse of vicious, criminal, deviant, ignorant, or undersocialized people".

Thus, "discontented men [and women] are more susceptible to conversion to new beliefs than contented ones".[110] But Gurr was unable to explain the micro foundations of this "conversion". Sometimes, he observed, that the question was answered by pointing to precipitating events – elections and their results, protests that descend into anger or the speeches of powerful demagogues. On other occasions, we blame insurrections on prejudices or bigotries – racism, xenophobia, anti-Semitism, white nationalism. I do not really want to take issue with Gurr.

What I want to do is simply to offer a social science explanation of the patterns that he identified at the macrolevel. At the risk of being labelled a "positivist", this book seeks to return to the ideal (or dream) of unified science espoused by the likes of Otto Neurath and the logical positivists between the World Wars.[111] He, in case you have never heard of him, was a famous sociologist who believed that all the social sciences could ultimately be reduced to a single science based on physics.

We should always draw on different perspectives. History provides one, psychology another and social neuroscience yet another. The latter, by combining political science and biology, studies the phenomenon of rebellion, not from empathetic considerations of what it is like to be in the shoes of a revolutionary, but one that looks at what happens in the brain when someone with the anger of a rebel is prompted to reach to external stimuli akin to those felt by insurrectionists.

In other words, neuropolitics studies what happens neurophysiologically in our heads when we engage in revolutions and rebellions.

So, from a social neuroscience perspective, why do people take part in insurrections, such as the January 6, 2021, attack on the US Capitol and the copycat attacks on the Brazilian Congress and the Supreme Court on January 8, 2023? Why do they engage in political violence from a neuroscience point of view?[112]

As we have also seen in other chapters of this book, I suggest that we think about insurrections as originating in our brains. Indeed, I'd suggest that the insurrections in Washington, D.C., and Brasília are due to overactivity in the amygdala – a primitive part of the brain that evolved millions of years ago, which we share with foxes and pigs.[113]

Social scientists used to focus on rational actions (as outlined in the introduction). But in recent years, we have made great advances in understanding what goes on in the brain when we think politically. The biology of radical politics is no exception.

Scholars have explored why people rebel for as long as there has been political science. In the early 1970s, one sociologist hypothesised that the reason was poverty, or "relative deprivation". Political scientists and economists, using sophisticated mathematical models, also tried to explain rebellion but found it hard to come up with a rational explanation. Very few people, the math showed, had any personal incentive to risk life and limb for the rather abstract benefits of overthrowing a government.

From a rational point of view, rebellions seem pointless. A political scientist even coined the phrase "the paradox of revolution".

Enter neuroscience. Since the early 2000s, when we, as the previous chapters have explained, have been able to look at what happens inside our heads when we think, we have also been able to understand what happens neurophysiologically when we rebel.

Using functional magnetic resonance imaging (fMRI) scans, which measure changes in blood flow to brain cells, we can now see which parts of the brain are activated when we engage in various activities, such as shopping, thinking about sex and feeling remorse.

As someone who, as previously mentioned, started out as a biologist before becoming a political scientist, what I personally found fascinating is how well these two areas go together. Those two different academic fields offer a similar lesson: to prevent rebellions and insurrections, we should avoid angry and polarised debate.

This perspective has also entered the realm of political analysis – finally putting the "science" in political science. Of course, fMRI isn't useful for studying rebellions in real time; there's no way to scan people's brains at the moment they storm the palace. But we can design experiments to observe how people who share insurrectionist views react to hate speech and to views articulated by politicians on the far right.

By presenting subjects with statements about vulnerable minority groups during some brain scan studies and showing them photos of political candidates they didn't agree with during others, researchers could literally see what happened in would-be insurrectionists' brains. Thus, when neurologist Giovanna Zamboni and colleagues conducted such an experiment a little over a decade ago, they discovered that a part of the brain known as the ventral striatum, which is associated with the limbic system, was activated when individuals (who were identified by psychological tests as "radicals") were exposed to hate-speech statements or other intolerant assertions about other groups or minorities. These studies have been replicated in recent years and their findings have been confirmed and refined.

That the ventral striatum was activated is remarkable. This part of the brain is one of the oldest in evolutionary terms. It is what makes animals respond positively to simple rewards in social situations and to negative stimuli in dangerous moments, such as the fear that they might be attacked. The ventral striatum is linked with the amygdala, the fight-and-flight centre in the brain. When people hear statements about – or see images of – groups or individuals that they fear, the brain reacts as if it were being attacked.

In contrast, study subjects who, based on personality tests, were identified as "moderate" or "conservative" used parts of the brain that have evolved only in humans, such as the dorsolateral prefrontal cortex, which is responsible for planning and working memory and is associated with listening, speaking and reasoning. In another study from 2011, young people with far-right views showed greater activation of the amygdala, indicating that they were less likely to reflect on political statements and more likely to revert to fight-or-flight mode.

The most interesting part of this body of research is that, generally, brains respond differently to politics than to policy. Scans show that when people think about politics – as in the bare-knuckle struggle – the fight-and-flight amygdala gets activated. But when people are exposed to questions about policy, they use the more advanced parts of the brain. In fMRI studies dating as far back as 2009, scientists found that the dorsolateral frontal cortex lit up in people exposed to arguments about economic policy.

As alluded to before, Aristotle, in 300 BC, believed that biology and politics go together. That is not a common view among scholars today. This view needs revision. For together, these two different academic fields offer a similar lesson: to prevent rebellions and insurrections, we should avoid angry and polarised debate. And when possible, we should avoid political hot-buttons and instead talk about the policy issues that affect our lives.

In *The Republic* and in some of his earlier dialogues, Plato talked about *Thymos* – often translated as spiritness.[114] This was not a negative thing entirely. There is a place for this feeling. Ideally, "the spirited part is the helper of reason by nature unless it is corrupted by bad upbringing".[115]

As Liya Yu, author of *Vulnerable Minds*, has put it, "emotions are an important part of politics": they "drive us onto the streets, [make us] oppose dictators, and make us protest". So, "the picture that social neuro social and political neuroscience paints for us is a much more complex one in which what we hitherto saw as irrational emotions." Thymos can be a wonderful thing if it is channelled towards higher things. In one of his earlier dialogues, Plato suggested that this spiritness "glorifies the achievements of the past and . . . teaches them to future generations".[116] But (and this was Plato's point) it can become destructive if citizens are animated by blind Thymos and follow a demagogue out of spite and anger. In these situations, Plato, through Socrates, concluded that Thymos would degenerate into a craze. The reason for this was that "madness can provide relief from the greatest plagues of trouble".[117] If you focus too much on that area, you are less likely to have defences in place if you develop Alzheimer's. If we revert to these parts, we partly deprive ourselves of the advantages we have gained through 8 million years of evolution, namely, the ability to listen and learn from discussion. But neuropolitics also shows something more positive.

Chapter 6
Neuromarketing and Its Discontents

"It is certain", said an article in *Forbes Magazine,* "that campaigns are using or plan to use neuromarketing as a tool to understand voter reactions and preferences, as well as evaluate campaign ads."[118]

Some might be shocked to hear this. After all, we don't like the idea that our democratic decisions are influenced by political consultants and spin doctors who manipulate our minds and make us vote for causes we do not support.

And yet, we may be deceiving ourselves if we entertain the thought that politics is a clean game where we are merely deciding whom to vote for after careful deliberation and weighing up preferences. Certainly, there is an element of this. But it cannot be denied that electoral politics is shaped by paid professionals.

In fact, a case could be made for the view that political consultants have existed for as long as democracy itself has. For example, the *Sophists,* made infamous by Plato, were arguably nothing but the political consultants of fifth-century BC Athens. Indeed, in his dialogue *Protagoras*, Plato explicitly defined a sophist as someone who "teaches how to realize one's maximum potential for success in political debate and action".[119] Plato's pupil Aristotle even wrote a whole treatise.

Other writers in this tradition include the Roman politician and philosopher Marcus Cicero, who wrote eloquently on the art of persuasion. And in a more practical vein, his brother Quintus Cicero wrote *Commentariolum Petitionis,* a detailed handbook for his brother's consular election campaign, complete with dirty tricks and cunning tactics based on rhetoric, such as casting doubt about the candidate's character.[120]

In the twentieth century, these tactics were finessed by the use of target polls, focus groups and the like. And, in recent years, political consultants have used AI and online targeting to find voters. For example, in the 2016 Brexit campaign, Victoria Woodcock – the operations director of *Vote Leave* – developed a new "canvassing software" that effectively identified voters who would potentially vote leave. Using this, the Brexiteer campaigners then asked members of the public to enter a competition where they could win £50 million if they could correctly identify the correct result of each of the fifty-one matches in the Euro 2016 soccer tournament. The only "price" for entering was to give Vote Leave their mobile number, email address and to answer how much on a scale from 1 to 10 the respondent hated the EU. Millions signed up. Drawing on this information, they signed up the Canadian-based company AggregateIQ to channel money to social media companies, "including $1.7 to Facebook for 146 m paid impressions. In total Vote Leave delivered 309m

 | https://doi.org/10.1515/9783111616506-007

online adds during the ten weeks [of official campaigning] and an impressive 890m Facebook impressions between October 2015 and 23 June 2016."[122]

This is not to get carried away writing about the dark arts of campaigning but merely to set the scene for this chapter in the story the emergence of neuromarketing.

But what can neuromarketing do? How does it work and how does it relate to general neuropolitics?

At the most fundamental level, neuromarketing utilises our knowledge of certain parts of the brain involved in inhibition (that dorsolateral prefrontal cortex again).

As is always the case with neuroscience, the lessons are drawn from a controlled experiment, which we subsequently try to extrapolate to a wider population.

Political consultants – for reasons outlined above – have been reluctant to share their insights. So before we try to discern them, let's start with an example from product advertising. Chocolate is a popular product. But are we likely to shift from Mars bars to Ritter? Or from Lindor to Cadbury?

Which is a better predictor of purchasing behaviour – qualitative research or fMRI scans? In a study, three German researchers subjected eighteen chocoholics (all women between the ages of 23 and 56) to a simple experiment.[123] The women were shown a photo of a Duplo bar (one of the best-selling German chocolate products) and six other products (including a toothbrush) for two seconds, followed by a three-second display of an ad for Duplo, then the product again for two seconds. After this, the women were asked to rank the products according to their preferences. The researchers were able to create three sales forecasts: one based on each of the women's stated preference, another based on brain activity while viewing the ads and finally one based on fMRI changes to product viewing before and after the marketing communications. The authors reported that "the fMRI imaging of participants during marketing communications (B) predicted sales (D) better than subjects' stated preference (A)".

Their other conclusion was "that ROIs [region of interest] consisting of NAcc, . . . [was] assumed to contribute positively to later sales DLPFC . . . [was] predicted to contribute negatively to sales".[124] Again, this is rather forbidding language, so let's break it down. In fact, it's all quite simple.

We need not focus on all the acronyms, only those the authors singled out as most important. The main ones the researchers drew attention to were NAcc and DLPFC. The latter – the dorsolateral prefrontal cortex – we have already met; it is the part of the brain associated with inhibition, one that we often see in people who are of a conservative persuasion.

The former stands for the *Nucleus Accumbens* – a part of the mid-brain deep below the surface of the frontal lobes. Now, what is interesting is that this part of the brain has been shown to be associated with the Pavlovian reflexes known in psychology.[125] The reader will recall that Pavlov's dog salivated when it associated the sound of a bell with food.

If we add to this the fact that the nucleus accumbens (henceforth, NAcc) is also associated with desire and motivation, it is probably not surprising that these parts of the brain were activated in those women who craved chocolate.

Nor is it surprising that the dorsolateral prefrontal cortex inhibits these responses in others.

What are we to make of this? Basically, advertisements can create a Pavlovian reflex that makes us (artificially) crave chocolate.

The big question is then whether a similar mechanism could be in play for political "tastes"? To answer this question, we need to look closer at the NAcc as part of the striatum (also known as the striate nucleus), a cluster of neurons in the so-called basal ganglia in the forebrain.

The striatum is an important component of what are known as the motor and reward systems.

So, can we see differences in different political persuasions? There are indications that we can. This has been succinctly put in a research paper on the neuropsychology of different Americans' brains. Jost and colleagues argue,

> Liberals have been found to exhibit increased brain activity and more grey matter volume in the anterior cingulate cortex, a brain region important for detecting cognitive conflict Furthermore, conservatives have been found to possess more grey matter volume in the amygdala, a region that detects motivationally salient objects, including threatening stimuli. These studies have helped to establish a growing body of research linking political beliefs and personality traits to specific neuropsychological and psychophysiological substrates.[126]

One of the findings of political science more generally is that negative advertising has an effect on party preferences. What is new is that this can be seen in brain scans as well. To understand this, we need to introduce one of these forbidding-sounding terms used by neuroscientists, in this case, the dorsolateral prefrontal cortex. This part of the brain is involved in decision-making[127] – which is why it has been of particular interest to economists using brain scans.[128]

Now, what is interesting in a political context is that "heightened dlPFC activity has been observed in those who change their candidate preferences in response to negative political advertising".[129] How exactly did this insight come about? The authors of the study carried out a simple experiment.

Eight women and 32 men were presented with videos from previous electoral campaigns and television commercials for major cola brands, and then used the subjects' self-rated affinity towards political candidates as behavioural indicators. After viewing negative campaign videos, subjects who showed stronger fMRI activation in the dorsolateral prefrontal cortex lowered their ratings of the candidate they had originally supported more than did those with smaller fMRI signal changes in the same region.[130]

But what was perhaps more interesting – at least from a political science perspective – was that the same negative effect could not be observed when the subjects were shown negative ads about brands of cola. What Figure 3 shows is that the signal change was negatively correlated with the previous preference for the politician. In other words, the greater the exposure to the advertisement, the lower the signal. Admittedly, the Pearson coefficient is relatively low at R = 0.33 (significant at p > 0.05), which is a medium correlation.

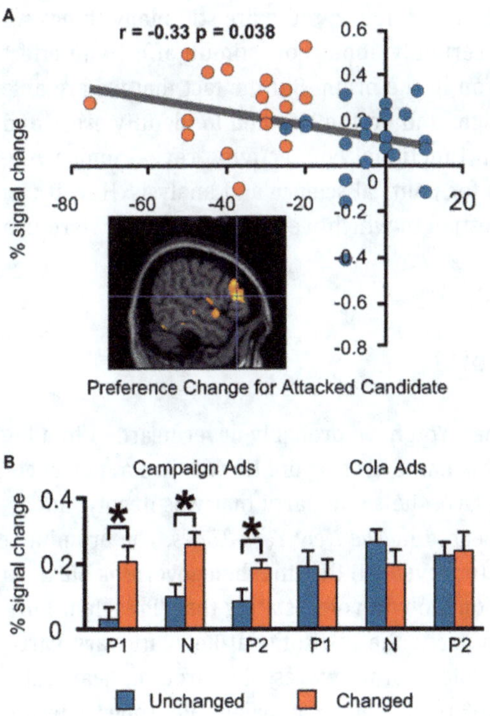

Figure 3: Signal change and preference for a political candidate and cola brand after negative ads. Source: Kato, J., Ide, H., Kabashima, I., Kadota, H., Takano, K., & Kansaku, K. (2009). Neural correlates of attitude change following positive and negative advertisements. *Frontiers in Behavioral Neuroscience*, *6*, 1.

Still, it shows something about neuropolitics that few were aware of – and, in any case, this correlation is as good as what we get in most sociological studies of political behaviour. If you look at the bar chart to the left, this offers a clearer impression of the differences between politics and beverages. As you can see, there is a massive change in the three columns representing negative ads about politicians – not so for the columns on the right, those representing two different coca brands.

So, the neuropolitical findings show a distinct effect for political ads, something, we might add, has been rather difficult to show using the conventional tools of political analysis.[131] What this research does, then, is not to render conventional political science and sociology methods redundant but to add another dimension to the process of mixed-methods triangulation that is essential in all path breaking research.

Admittedly, the research is still in its infancy; there are still many things we do not know about the brain, and certainly about how stimuli affect and effect the physiological processes that go on in the brain. But the fact that we are able to detect when people are on the right and on the left, and to identify areas and regions of the cortex that, through functional connectivity, reveal underlying preferences is a giant step forward for political science and analysis. How it can be used and often abused is the question to which we now turn to. So, we return again to neuropolitics.

Neuropolitics in the Real World

His name was Manlio Fabio Beltrones. You have probably never heard of him before. And you are unlikely to hear his name ever again. He was just a messenger working for a political party in Mexico, the same party that was deeply embarrassed by a revelation that had appeared in *The New York Times*. The prominent American newspaper had reported (or revealed) that the then governing Mexican party had used neuropolitics technique to win votes, stating that "President Enrique Peña Nieto's campaign and his party, the Institutional Revolutionary Party, or PRI, employed tools to measure voters' brain waves, skin arousal, heart rates and facial expressions during the 2012 presidential campaign". Beltrones vowed it would never happen again. For ever more, the party "would stick to tried and trusted campaign tools, like polls and political intuition", and rely on "the old-fashioned way" in its "future campaigns", he told the American paper.[132]

A story like this would seem rather mundane and unimportant. From our perspective, it is not.

In the light of what we have seen in previous chapters, PRI had not been particularly sophisticated. They had merely used research that neuropolitics pioneers had developed a decade before. The scientists' research had focused on the amygdala, by now the familiar and evolutionarily very old part of the brain, which, as the reader will by now know, is, *inter alia*, associated with fear and fight responses.

What the researchers had found, using fMRI scans, was that "the human amygdala processes both the degree of emotion in facial expressions and the categorical ambiguity of the emotion shown".[133] This little piece of information was rather creatively picked up by PRI. They wanted to know whether the impressions of their candidates would prompt different facial expressions, which – albeit indirectly – could help them gauge the voters' propensity to vote PRI.

If I were to explain it to you, it would go something like this: the amygdala responds in a particular way, and this is shown in the facial expressions. The Mexican party officials and their advisors found this very useful, not least if you try to find out how a campaign slogan works.

So, what did the Mexicans do in practice? At the entrance to several buildings, there was a photo of the candidate, but there was a secret camera behind it, which recorded these by-passers' expressions and, presto, PRI could determine whether the candidate inspired trust – or not!

Not brain scans, to be sure, but research based on findings from neuropolitics nonetheless.

PRI promised to mend their ways. This is the usual pattern. Political campaigns and parties have always been reluctant to admit to using such dark arts, including but not limited to hidden surveillance.

But the protestations of the PRI notwithstanding, the techniques have not gone away from Mexican political campaigning. In any case, it is certainly interesting that Vladimir Humberto Herrera Aquino, a Mexican political advisor, a few years later, wrote an article which in English translates to "Neuropolitics, a new way to win elections".[134]

If unseen forces steer us, this book forces you to ask who's holding the wheel.

Before we can do so, however, we need to pause and look at the brain science of political behaviour and where we are up to. To get an overview of where we are in regard to the various centres of the brain that are associated with political thinking, the work of political psychologist Drew Westen is a good place to start. In a book about a decade ago, he wrote:

> Roughly speaking, two broad regions of the prefrontal cortex are worth discussing [from a political point of view]. Towards the top and side of the frontal lobes is the dorsolateral prefrontal cortex . . . this part of the brain is always active when people make conscious

> choices . . . The other region of the prefrontal cortex, peering out from behind the eyes, and extending about halfway up the forehead, is the ventromedial prefrontal cortex . . . [It is] involved in social and emotional experience, social and emotional intelligence, and moral functioning. It also plays a crucial role in linking thoughts and emotion, particularly in using reactions to guide decision making. Not surprisingly, this region has dense neural connections with cerebral structures below the cortex involved in generation emotional states, such as amygdala.[135]

Professor Westen was overtly liberal and proudly declared his political affiliation. This is commendable. Being a partisan does not automatically mean that you are wrong or that your conclusions are untrustworthy. The neuropsychologist found it "tempting to map our current political topography onto these two regions of the prefrontal cortex".[136]

He suggested that Democrats were more likely to draw on the dorsolateral prefrontal cortex, whereas Republicans were more emotional and were guided more by excitements and gut feelings rather than rational reasoning.

Nearly 20 years on, we know this is an oversimplification. Indeed, there are indications that the dorsolateral prefrontal cortex lights up in the brains of conservatives, as this part of the brain is also associated with inhibition and caution – traits that are associated with being on the right of the political spectrum.

That Professor Westen got it somewhat wrong is not an accusation of bias. It is part of good scientific practice. As good researchers know, we make scientific progress not through verification but by learning from mistakes; by putting forward theories that can be refuted, that is, which we gradually modify to get a more accurate picture of reality.[137]

So, given that neuroscience moves on and learns from its mistakes like any other proper science, what is the state of our knowledge today? What are the theories yet to be falsified? And how do they pertain to neuropolitics?

A famous American neuroscientist named John Jost has come up with a somewhat nerdy phrase called "the motivated social cognition model". He is allowed to do that. Such phrasing may seem alienating to non-scientists, but it serves a purpose for researchers. Anyway, his model essentially says that holding conservative views is a way of coping with threats. Thus, "chronically and temporarily activated needs to reduce uncertainty, ambiguity, threat, and disgust . . . are positively associated with conservatism".[138] You probably don't need a degree in sociology to come up with that. Indeed, there are any number of perceptive and impressive ethnographic studies that reach this conclusion based on participant observation and qualitative studies, such as Hochschild's sociological study *Strangers in Their Own Land.*[139]

One of the conclusions from these studies of those who voted for President Trump, and those who voted for Brexit in the UK and other "populist" causes was that they were perceived to be under threat. What we are interested in, from a social neuroscience perspective, is how this manifests itself in the brain. Not, mind you, because we believe in some kind of reductionism, but because this perspective complements the more traditional social science and humanities perspective.

So what do we know? Certainly, other scholars have come to some of the same conclusions. Whether conservative or not, it is a consistent finding that "emotion, decision making and the orbitofrontal cortex" are associated when people make political choices.[140]

But can this research make a difference? And how does it compare to traditional political science? Well, for starters, neuropolitics has presented some rather remarkable findings. For example, that we can predict individuals' ideology with 85% accuracy.[141] If you contrast this to tried and tested ways of gauging people (generally based on their parents' political leanings), this is a rather impressive figure. The old methods only predict ideology with 65% accuracy. Yes, you ought to be impressed.

Yet some are unconvinced and have said that these researchers are "overstating the definitiveness of its theoretical implications".[142] That might always be the case, and especially if we are basing these conclusions on a small number of studies, but when the same results point in the same direction, and when the initial findings are being corroborated, these criticisms become more difficult to sustain.

Using so-called "multidimensional scaling and parametric functional magnetic resonance imaging to identify which criteria/dimensions people use to structure complex political beliefs and which brain regions are concurrently activated", Zambioni and colleagues:

> Found that three independent dimensions explained the variability of a set of statements expressing political beliefs and that each dimension was reflected in a distinctive pattern of neural activation: individualism (medial prefrontal cortex and temporoparietal junction), conservatism (dorsolateral prefrontal cortex), and radicalism (ventral striatum and posterior cingulate). The structures we identified are also known to be important in self–other processing, social decision-making in ambivalent situations, and reward prediction. Our results extend current knowledge on the neural correlates of the structure of political beliefs, a fundamental aspect of the human ability to coalesce into social entities.[143]

This might require a bit of explanation. What this study basically shows is that those who are conservative activate the dorsolateral prefrontal cortex, which is associated with caution – in line with the findings by Jost (see above). Conservatives, as the term implies, are guarded and want things to stay the same. So it stands to reason that they activate a part of the brain that is also associated with an aversion to risk-taking.[144]

What is also interesting is that radicals – those who are more likely to support populist policies and are driven more by the activation of the more evolutionary primitive parts of the brain – are more likely to go for what we might call instant gratification. The reported findings that these activated the ventral striatum are interesting. This part of the so-called basal ganglia (a structure under the surface) is widely reported to be involved in "social comparison on reward processing in the human brain".[145]

But the evidence, in fairness, is not totally conclusive, and there are subtle differences. A study that received considerable press – at least within neuropolitics circles – was "Political Orientations are correlated with brain structure in young adults". The reason why this paper got more than its fair share of attention was that one of the co-authors was the Hollywood actor Colin Firth. In a way, it is slightly unfortunate for the man who played Mr. Darcy in *Bridged Jones's Diary* and in the BBC's adaptation of *Pride and Prejudice* was co-author of a study that moved the dial of neuropolitical research.[146]

In the study, the researchers found that "Substantial differences exist in the cognitive styles of liberals and conservatives on psychological measures". Thus, in a sample of young adults, the researchers related self-reported political attitudes to grey matter volume using structural MRI and found that "greater liberalism was associated with increased grey matter volume in the Anterior Cingulate Cortex".[147]

This, again, needs to be explained. The anterior cingulate cortex is a part of the brain that lies at the front part of the central sulcus, the valley that separates the two cerebral hemispheres. This part of the cerebrum has been shown in other studies to be associated with empathy,[148] which might be consistent with the tendency of liberal and more socialist voters to have a greater sense of social justice and concern for the least well-off.[149]

But Firth and colleagues also found something that may be similar to what we saw in the previous chapter on populism. They found that "greater conservatism was associated with increased volume of the right amygdala",[150] a part of the brain that is – as we have seen – associated with more visceral responses. That these findings were subsequently "replicated in an independent sample of additional participants", needless to say, make them more trustworthy.

Yet, as good researchers, Firth and colleagues acknowledged that we have to be cautious and duly admitted that their "data do not determine whether these regions play a causal role in the formation of political attitudes, they converge with previous work to suggest a possible link between brain structure and psychological mechanisms that mediate political attitudes".

By linking their findings to earlier studies showing something along the same lines, they clearly corroborated their findings. Thus, their work showed something that had been found in cross-cultural studies – as they pointed out in the article.

One of the arguments against traditional social science and philosophy is that it is biased and reflects Western norms and cultures. Political science, *qua* a social science developed to analyse voters and politicians in American and European societies, may not be good at understanding and analysing individuals who do not live in these societies.

The same criticism could be levelled at neuropolitics, except that some of the findings suggest that these patterns are of cross-cultural validity. This, certainly, was the conclusion of a study that compared American and Japanese voters. Rule and colleagues found that candidates for whom participants from both countries chose to vote for "elicited stronger responses in the bilateral amygdala than candidates for whom participants chose not to vote", and that this finding was "true regardless of either the participant's culture or the target's culture", something which suggested that "these voting decisions provoked the same neural response cross-culturally".[151] So when Darren Schreiber and colleagues were able to observe differences between the "red" and the "blue" brains, they were not just reporting on an American phenomenon. The same pattern is seen in other places too – even if more research is needed to draw firmer conclusions.[152]

So, in terms of identifying patterns, neuropolitics arguably has an edge in being able to provide findings that transcend cultural differences – albeit within developed capitalist societies. But can we trust these findings more generally? And isn't it a problem that all these studies were based on self-reported political identification?

Well, there is a way of overcoming this. Psychologists have developed a so-called Implicit Association Test (IAT) to, as it were, say what we really think about race, gender stereotypes and such like.[153]

In a study that is often cited in the emerging literature on neuropolitics, Knutzon and colleagues "assessed political attitudes using the IAT in which participants were presented with faces and names of well-known Democrat and Republican politicians along with positive and negative words while undergoing functional MRI". They "found a significant behavioral IAT effect for the face of the politician".[154] In particular, they found that "amygdala and fusiform gyrus were activated during perceptual processing of familiar faces" (the fusiform gyrus is a large area in the lower part of the temporal cortex, which plays important roles in object and face recognition, so, this is not, in itself, surprising).[155]

But what was more interesting from a political science point of view was that "Frontopolar activation was positively correlated with an implicit measure of bias . . . (how strongly the participants felt about the politicians), while strength of affiliation with political party was negatively correlated with lateral Prefrontal Cortex", which, in their view, gave credence to the "idea that two distinct but interacting networks, one emphasizing rapid, stereotypic, and emotional associative knowledge and the other emphasizing more deliberative and factual knowledge co-operate in the processing of politicians". Thus, when evaluating politicians, we are driven by gut feelings but also, occasionally, if we like them, by more reasoned thinking.

Now, this is all well, but it rather risks stating the bleedingly obvious. To say that we sometimes are biased and sometimes base our decisions on deliberation is not really that path-breaking. What we need to show is when we do the former rather than the latter.

So, an obvious question would be: When are we biased? When is it that, say, a photo of a politician elicits an emotional response that can be detected by an activated amygdala in an fMRI scan? This is exactly the question Michael Spezio and colleagues set out to investigate in their study, "A neural basis for the effect of candidate appearance on election outcomes".[156]

But they also found that "images of losing candidates . . . elicited greater activation in the insula and ventral anterior cingulate".[157] Why exactly this is so is less obvious. Insula is an area associated with empathy, and the ventral anterior cingulate cortex is associated with social evaluation.[158] This piece of research could suggest that we feel sorry for losers. In this age of hate speech, this could be a nice touch, but it is not something we can conclusively prove.

Does all this give us a positive view of politics? Is it good to be politically involved? Most of us would think so.

Not long after leaving university, I landed a job in the British Home Office. At the time, this was the UK ministry that was responsible for elections. The minister – the Home Secretary – at the time was David Blunkett, a man who never took prisoners, let alone suffered fools gladly, was a robust and impressive Yorkshireman who had overcome Dickensian poverty and his blindness to become one of the most influential men in the country.

For him, it was politics and political engagement that had taken him from Dickensian poverty in Sheffield to power in SW1. As I recall him saying, "interest in politics is always a good thing. We must do everything we can to get people involved in politics, get them to vote. That is the start of any civilized and democratic society."

It is difficult to disagree with this sentiment. But the findings of neuropolitics somewhat qualify the panacea-like fervour of Mr Blunkett. In fact, some of the findings rather suggest that too much political interest might not be so great after all.

This, at any rate, is what Marta Gozzi and colleagues find in the paper titled "Interest in politics modulates neural activity in the amygdala and ventral striatum".[159]

They "scanned individuals (either interested or uninterested in politics based on a self-report questionnaire) while they were expressing their agreement or disagreement with political opinions". After the scanning, "participants were asked to rate each political opinion presented in the scanner for emotional valence and emotional intensity". What they found was, rather alarmingly (if you agree with Blunkett's view), that "individuals interested in politics showed greater activation in the amygdala and the ventral striatum (ventral putamen) relative to individuals uninterested in politics when reading political opinions in accordance with their own views".[160] And they concluded that "this study shows that having an interest in politics elicits activations in emotion- and reward-related brain areas even when simply agreeing with written political opinions".[161]

By this stage, the reader should be able to draw conclusions from this study, at least as far as the amygdala is concerned. As we have seen in the previous chapter, and in the abovementioned study by Firth and colleagues, the amygdala is activated when people are angry and fearful – and it is a part of the brain that is – in evolutionary perspective – rather primitive. So, to put it crudely, those who are interested in politics are not necessarily the most cerebral; they rely on gut feelings and not necessarily on deliberation.

But the study also found that the ventral striatum (in particular, the ventral putamen) was activated. What does this mean? And what is this part of the brain known for?

The ventral putamen (ventral here stands for the Latin "belly-side") is part of the basal ganglia, which we have already encountered. It is, again, put rather crudely, a part of the reward system. That is not a problem, of course; rewards are an important part of a healthy psychological process. Indeed, the putamen is involved in learning and motor control, including speech articulation, language functions, reward and cognitive functioning.[162] But it is also involved in addiction, and is associated with some less attractive traits, such as obsessive gambling.[163] The putamen, combined with the globus pallidus, forms the lentiform nucleus, and with the caudate nucleus, it shapes the striatum, which is a subcortical structure that forms the basal ganglia.

So, the fact – if we are to believe Gozzi et al. – that those interested in politics really show greater activation of the centres of the brain associated with addiction and aggression is not a great advertisement for political engagement.

As it happens, this is not a new or exceptional finding. In the 1960s, political sociologists Almond and Verba suggested that political systems work best if people are not constantly engaged in politics. They espoused – based on interviews with voters – a so-called civic culture in which citizens did not deplete their "civic reserves" but kept them in store for when things went wrong.[164] In a way, this finding chimes with – and is supported by – the recent findings of neuropolitics.

So, can all this knowledge be used in practical politics? Say, to win elections? Perhaps that is the wrong question. Perhaps these techniques have already been used. Certainly, the example from Mexico cited at the beginning of this chapter seems to indicate this.

These are the negatives, or so you may perceive them. But could all this neuropolitics business be a force for good? Is there light somewhere at the end of the tunnel or just darkness?

Chapter 7
How Social Neuroscience Can Help Combat Racism

Here is a story from the real world, and a bloody brutal one at that:

> He never stood a chance. His first mistake was looking for food alone; perhaps things would have turned out differently if he'd been with someone else. The second, bigger mistake was wandering too far up the valley into a dangerous wooded area. This was where he risked running into the Others, the ones from the ridge above the valley. At first, there were two of them, and he tried to fight, but another four crept up behind him and he was surrounded. They left him there to bleed to death and later returned to mutilate his body. Eventually, nearly 20 such killings took place, until there was no one left, and the Others took over the whole valley.[165]

So started an article in the famous *Foreign Affairs* magazine. You could be excused for thinking that this was a tale from the Peloponnesian War, in which "the weak suffer they must", as the historian of that conflict wrote.[166] Or maybe it was a brutal scene from the Rwanda genocide in 1994. In fact, it was neither.

Although it happened in a place geographically close to the latter, the victim, as it happens, was not even human. He was a chimpanzee. The male chimps in one – should we call it ethnic – group systematically kill neighbouring males, kidnap the surviving females and expand their territory. Just like humans do. The author of the article even cites some chimp-criminology, and notes that our nearest evolutionary relatives are about thirty times as likely to kill someone from a neighbouring group as they are to kill some one from their own tribe. On average, eight males gang up on the victim.

We share 98% of our DNA with chimpanzees. So maybe it is not really surprising that humans also divide the world into "us" and "them", and that we too can be cruel, vicious and inhumane. But there is a difference. We are endowed with rationality and reason to a degree that these primates do not. So might we be able to persuade people not to pursue the hatred that gave rise to the chimp murder, and maybe, social neuroscience could play a role in this? For if we know for certain what parts of the brain get activated by specific stimuli (advertisements, infomercials and the like), we may be able to persuade people in a positive way and convince them not to engage in hate crimes, racism and other forms of discrimination. This may seem a vain hope. The following pages will show something else.

 | https://doi.org/10.1515/9783111616506-008

Neuro-sociobiology

We have already touched upon the now-discredited pseudoscience of phrenology. Much in vogue in the Victorian age, adherents of it believed that small bumps in the head could reveal underlying brain structures, and you could tell if a person was honest, modest and prudish by measuring the skull. Even Queen Victoria was a believer (her children all had their crania measured).

It was soon disgraced. Much in the same way as palm-reading and astrology. But unlike these, elements of it persisted, and while lumps on the head could tell us nothing, there was evidence that certain parts of the brain are indeed responsible for different thoughts and activities.

Fast-forward nearly a hundred years, and the Canadian neurologist Wilder Penfield relied on other traumas in the brain to locate other parts of the brain that were responsible for thought, behaviour and other things, including consciousness.[167] He worked with Barbara Milner, whom we met in Chapter 1.

In its own way, this was a little bit revolutionary. Philosophers (and many other people) had believed there was a difference between the body and the soul and that somehow our thoughts were a mystical entity that was somehow immaterial.[168] Whatever religious or philosophical consequences you may want to draw from this are a personal matter.

Up to this point, all the research had relied on unfortunate souls (no pun intended) who had suffered trauma to the brain. It goes without saying that such lesions are rather random. Experiments had been carried out to measure the electrical activity in the brain. This technique, known as electroencephalography (EEG), it could detect activity in the brain, but it was imprecise. The quantum leap forward was functional magnetic resonance imaging (or fMRI scans).

Let us just repeat some of the basics of the research method, just in case you need a refresher. Without boring you with unnecessary details, this is a technique based on the well-known fact that blood is, in large measure, composed of iron atoms. And this metal, as we all know, is magnetic. If we assume that blood flows to the part of the brain that is activated (as these areas need oxygen to function), then it stands to reason that a scan would reveal the parts of the brain that have the most iron in them. Because it is basically measuring blood and oxygen, it is technically known as “BOLD” imaging (it stands for *blood-oxygenation-level-dependent imaging*).

So, when you show someone, for example, a photo of someone they dislike, a part of the brain responsible for hate will need more oxygenated blood, and this will show up in the scanner, and we can – to a degree – read the person’s mind. Okay, I am simplifying a bit, but not more than researchers do when they explain it in textbooks. In crude terms, what we are doing is a mix between political science and brain science. You may still have reservations about this. To mix biology with politics is a tricky issue, and it is not the way political science has been carried out over the past 100 years, let alone the last 2300 years to be honest.

But maybe that is about to change. Certainly, there are biologists who have thought about politics in ways that are interesting to social scientists. Some of them actually predated the emergence of neuropolitics. It might be useful to have a look at them. Let's once more get back to basics.

You might object that humans can solely be understood through the prism of science. Surely, we are more advanced. Surely, sociology, not biology, is key to understanding human behaviour. In fact, the very first political scientist, our old friend, Aristotle, explicitly called us a *zoon politikon* – literally a "political animal" – because he realised that we are literally "animals". The ancient Greek (he was actually Macedonian) thinker was also a gifted biologist (and even founded this discipline). But when dealing with our species, he was using his insights from science to understand politics.

This way of looking at things was more or less abandoned in the Renaissance, under the influence of so-called humanist thinkers. But it re-emerged in the twentieth century. Sociologists began to use analogies of the human body to explain how societies functioned. And the biologist Edward O. Wilson took a step further and coined the term *sociobiology*[169] and defined the new discipline as "the extension of population biology and evolutionary theory to social organization".[170]

Wilson had written seminal books on ants and had shown that the little social animals were anything but. Biologists – especially those specialising in insects like Wilson – took the view that wars and other forms of aggression without seeming motivation were something that characterised many species. Chimpanzees were one example. So too were ants.[171] So maybe we are just like ants and chimps; maybe we were born – literally – inhumane?

But, of course, there is one difference. At least now. Back in the day, say in the 1930s, it was acceptable to be prejudicial. Even great and admired philosophers expressed uninhibited racist views. Immanuel Kant, for one, wrote that Native Americans have "by nature no feeling that rises above the ridiculous".[172] He also wrote elsewhere that they are "incapable of all culture".[173]

After the end of colonialism and the genocides of the twentieth century, to utter such things was simply not acceptable. Today, few people admit to being racists. Still, some people harbour thoughts they wouldn't say in public. And, occasionally, people express views to their close circles that display worrying signs of Islamophobia, homophobia and antisemitism.

You probably agree with me that we need to do everything to combat this. I hope so, anyway. But you may ask: Is it really that bad? Aren't racism and antisemitism things of the past? Social statistics, sadly, indicate that they are not. One statistic will suffice. It comes courtesy of a report by *Reuters*:

> Hate crimes in England and Wales rose by 25 percent in the year ending March 2024, primarily driven by an increase in anti-Jewish offences following the outbreak of the Israel-Hamas conflict last October, official data showed on Thursday. The interior ministry said the number of offences recorded by police as motivated by a person's religion or perceived religion rose to 10,484 from 8,370 the previous year.[174]

These figures, alongside similar statistics for other kinds of phobia, are, of course, sad in every way. But might these figures even be misrepresenting reality? Might things be even worse?

You will not be surprised to hear that social neuroscience has an answer to this, which we will, of course, return to shortly. But traditional psychology has an answer, too. And, in some ways, the two go together. Psychologists have developed what is known as the *Implicit Association Test* (IAT, we have already used this technique, so here is another refresher).

It is, to put it in layman's terms, a way of understanding what you "really" think about minority groups, gays, other races, etc. These would – and will – often reveal themselves in subconscious associations between the way we see other people and how we react.[175]

The scary – and sad – thing is that most people, even when they say they are tolerant, are anything but. This is what a researcher found when she sent out a questionnaire to people. The data showed something else. Even if people did not admit to being racists, the results of the IAT revealed that – subconsciously – they were.

People associated Black people – in this example – with negative traits, whereas they had positive associations when they were shown images of White (Caucasian) people.

So far, so reprehensible. But the researchers went one step further. Instead of just subjecting these closet racists (for this is what they were) to a psychological test, they also employed social neuroscience. At the time when the study was carried out, fMRI scans (which measure the blood oxygenation and hence indicate which parts of the brain are activated) had more or less just been invented.

So, they were breaking new ground when they put people in an fMRI scanner for the next experiment. It divided into two. First, the individuals who had participated in the IAT underwent brain scanning, and then they were shown photos of people from a different racial group.

In both cases, the by now familiar part of the brain called the amygdala was, among other centres, activated. So, when they heard or read the statements about Black fellow citizens, their amygdala was activated. More interestingly, when people saw photos or films of people of a different race, their eyes were startled, and, once again, their amygdala was activated.

What is the significance of this, you may ask? You may or may not know that the amygdala has been called the "fear and fight" centre of the brain. It is never quite as simple as that. Nothing is simple in social neuroscience. But it is certainly the case that "clinical observations suggest that humans with amygdala damage have abnormal fear reactions and a reduced experience of fear".[176] The amygdala is not part of the cerebral cortex, which is the higher site of the more advanced functions of the brain, let alone the "thinking parts of the brain", which are mainly located in the frontal lobes. It is a part of the brain we share with many other, less advanced, animals. It is largely instinctive. So, when we see a rattlesnake or when someone runs towards us with an axe, the amygdala kicks in and adapts a defensive position even when we are not fully cognisant of this. So, it is concerning that people unconsciously react in this way when they see faces of different colours.

Social neuroscience is a complex business. And it is important that this research is not simplified too much. When these experiments are carried out, other parts of the brain are, of course, activated, too. Merely looking at things means that we activate the occipital regions towards the back of the brain, simply because this is where visual inputs are processed.

What you should be interested in are the other, if you like, "thinking" parts that show up on fMRI scans when you see photos and films. One of them is the so-called insula. As the Latin name implies, this is an island of grey matter on the side of the brains, under the flap beneath the temples.

So, why is this so interesting? Sadly, this is because this part of the brain – among many other things – is responsible for feelings of disgust.[177] So, it is not only that these people feel threatened and fearful (which activates the amygdala) when they see Black people; they are also showing signs of outright disgust. They probably wouldn't admit to this. I hope not. But the scans, so to speak, don't lie.

Another part of the brain that showed up in the scans is the right anterior cingulate cortex. This part lies in the valley in the frontal part of the brain. Does that change the conclusion that these people were, so to speak, hardwired to be racist? Yes, it does, a little bit. The ACC (as it is known to brain scientists) is a part that deals with many things. It is involved with empathy and feeling other people's pain. But it also shows up in scans when subjects are involved in what is known as affect-regulation, which is another way of saying the ability to control and manage uncomfortable emotions.[178] Perhaps we can see this as an unconscious admission of guilt? Or, perhaps less dramatically, as the brain's recognition that disgust and fear of other races are something socially unacceptable, something has to be kept within the socially acceptable norms. So, the ACC's activation is really just a way of glossing over racism. So, not good, really.

I hope you share my view that something needs to be done about this. But what?

Perhaps, and I am not entirely facetious, we could take an anti-racism pill? I am using this example because an experiment by Oxford University actually found that taking a drug called propranolol reduces implicit negative racial bias.[179] This drug is a so-called beta-blocker, one that is often given to people who suffer from chest pain, high blood pressure, heart rhythm disorders and implicit racism.

But here we obviously have to get real. Yes, racism – and implicit bias – is a "disease", but it is not one that can be treated like the common cold, cholera or constipation. It is unrealistic, and probably undesirable too, to prescribe pills for the mass of the population who have negative scores on IAT.

So, is there anything else we can do? Or is it just a (tragic) fact of life that we feel prejudice towards people with a different skin colour, ethnic background or religious affiliation?

For a long time, scholars and researchers (grudgingly) conceded the point that a lot of people were ill-disposed towards other people. For example, in the early 2000s, psychologists from the University of Chicago sent out over 4,000 CVs to employers in Boston and Chicago. The results confirmed the negative suspicion. Those with typical American names like Emily or Greg were called to interviews. Those with names that sounded "ethnic" like Lakisha and Jamal, did not. There were 50% more call-backs for those with Caucasian-sounding names – even if they had the same qualifications.[180]

Tobacco on Your Brain

You don't have to be an accountant to know that there are limited resources. So it stands to reason that we want to know whether money is well spent on information campaigns. Throwing good money after bad, especially if it is the taxpayers', is never a good idea. This was the problem that faced the National Cancer Institute's helpline. The good folks at the NCI wanted to help smokers quit. But how?

Well, with ads, of course.

They had devised three campaigns, which they – not being very imaginative – called A, B and C. But to be on the safe side, they asked members of a focus group to rank them according to efficiency. When they tested the messages in focus groups of smokers, the answer came back as B, A and then C.

Now, some people have expressed concern that these techniques may not work quite as effectively as was once believed. In fact, after two decades plus, some believed this approach to understanding public opinion and preferences was rather useless.[181] So, the National Cancer Institute went old-school elitist. They asked a group of marketing experts which of the ads was the best and most effective. The answer was the same: B, followed by A and then C. This would normally have settled the matter, except that the NCI were a diligent bunch. So they consulted a social neuroscientist and her team. Emily Falk and her collaborators had already carried out research on addiction and information campaigns. In these studies, they had analysed brain scans of people's responses to statements about smoking and alcohol,[182] so they seemed an appropriate choice. In these studies, they found that the ventromedial prefrontal cortex (the area on the illustration marked in purple; see Figure 4) – the part of the brain associated with self-evaluation and behaviour changes – was activated when people watched different video clips.

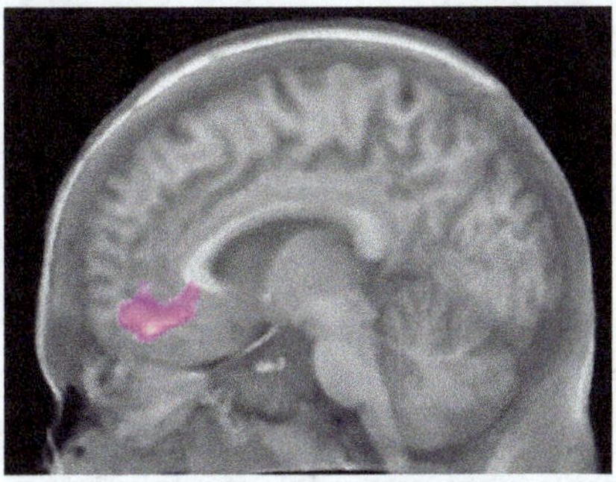

Figure 4: Video brain.
Source: Phelps, E. A., et al. (2000). Performance on indirect measures of race evaluation predicts amygdala activation. *Journal of Cognitive Neuroscience*, *12*(5), 729–738.

They followed the same format when they analysed the NCI informational ads.[183] But here is the thing: when the researchers carried out their fMRI scans, the order was different. The activation of the vmPFC was highest for C, followed by B and then A.

Of course, this could just indicate that the social neuroscience results were not so good after all, you might say? Or something else? How could we find out?

The researchers had a good idea. They tracked the number of people who rang the 1-800-QUIT-NOW helpline after each of the ads had aired. After all, ringing a helpline was a good proxy-measure of how effective it was. So which ad was the most effective?

You will probably not be surprised to hear that the order was C – B – A, exactly as predicted by the neuroscientists. So, based on this quite ingenious experiment, it seems that neuromarketing works. Of course, "One swallow maketh not summer", as the old saying goes, and a single study is just that, while earlier studies have been less conclusive.[184] But still, that a small study of 32 individuals could better predict the effectiveness of an ad-campaign that could benefit skilled professionals and smokers themselves is worth writing home about.

Actually, we should not be too concerned about the sample size. In another study conducted by some of the same researchers, they were able to predict how people would react to anti-smoking messages. Fifty subjects were placed under the brain scanner and were asked to react to images. When they did so, there was similar activation in the medial prefrontal cortex. When 400,000 people were shown the same images, they chose the same images.

In statistics, there is a measure of this association. It is called Pearson's Correlation, or R. A perfect association is 1.00 – and none is 0. Normally, a high correlation is R = 0.5. In this case, rather amazingly, the statistical model the researchers developed was able to predict the behaviour of the large sample size with 80% certainty. So, even a small sample can be used to forecast large-scale behaviour.[185]

So might this be used in other areas? And could it be that more objective information is better than scaremongering?

It is easy to be cynical about advertising and information campaigns. Often, the default position is to go for sensationalism instead of cerebral approaches. Just think of the ubiquitous campaigns against smoking, such as the one I already told you about.

People urged to kick the habit are subjected to endless graphic pictures of rotting teeth, bleeding ulcers and cancer-infested lungs. But do scaremongering campaigns work? The researchers who carried out the study for the NCI didn't go into detail. So the question remains: Are people more susceptible to public health campaigns based on solid evidence and advice? This question has remained unanswered for years.

Now, social neuroscience can shed light on it. And the findings are surprising. In a paper published in the journal *Neuroimage*, Daniel D. Langleben scanned people who watched, respectively, scare campaigns and neutral images.

He found that, neurologically speaking, emotive campaigns only activated parts of the brain in the visual cortex. However, when people were shown information-rich videos, they activated the higher parts of the brain, such as the orbitofrontal cortex – a part of the frontal lobes associated with emotion, reward value and reward-related decision-making.

In addition to this, those exposed to information-rich public service statements activate their hippocampus – the part in the midbrain that is associated with memory. The reverse is not the case with sensationalist, scaremongering campaigns.[186]

So, from the point of view of social neuroscience, education works – scare-mongering does not.

Could this be the key to educating people about the curse of antisemitism? Could it be that actual information campaigns work better than the messages focusing on emotional appeal?

In other words, would it be that neutral campaigns with factual information are better at literally educating people about the hatred towards a specific minority group? Could social neuroscience help us craft messages?

The answer would seem to be in the affirmative. Falk and her colleagues' experiments confirmed Langleben's results: "evidence demonstrates that activity within brain systems associated with self-related processing can predict individual behaviour in response to health messages".[187]

However, it could be objected that these results have only been shown to work on televised ads. Given that only 48% of Gen Z watch television,[188] are these findings at all useful in today's media landscape?

One argument could be that many of these users watch full-length video messages on platforms like TikTok and Instagram. Statistics show that "video content had risen to 82 percent of the total content on all social media platforms by the end of 2022" and that it is "roughly 15 times higher compared to the statistics of 2017!"[189]

In fact, this is supported by more recent research. In a paper published in the journal *Behavioural Sciences*, Hedda Šola and colleagues found evidence of an "untapped potential of neuromarketing in online learning".[190]

Like in other marketing, influence is based on the two-step hypothesis. Harking back to a famous study in the 1940s, marketing research has been based on the idea that the so-called "opinion former's" (people whom others listen to) are influenced by ads, and that their views, in turn, affect others.[191] This model, as you have probably already guessed, is identical to the now-commonplace view that "influencers" have an impact on how we see the world.[192]

As usual, a bit of background is useful for those who may not have studied social psychology.

Until Lazarsfeld and colleagues carried out their famous study in Erie County in 1940,[193] it was widely believed that people who received messages would conform to the injection model. In short, they would respond to infomercials and adverts as if they were injected with information into their mental bloodstream. This, however, turned out not to be the case. Rather, it was a two-step process. Using the sociological concept of primary groups, they proposed that we are all part of an intimate circle of people, and that we delegate cognitive tasks to other, better-informed individuals in our network. For example, if I don't have time to follow the latest developments in the Premier League, I turn to my friend Dan, who will tell me all about it. Likewise, my friend Em will tell me what I need to know about celebrities and dogs, and my good friend Theo will bring me up to speed on matters related to the Vatican and American political history. And yes, you get the drift.[194] The point is that we delegate because we can't know everything.

When social media and algorithms became a thing in the first decade of the 2000s, it was widely assumed that the injection model worked, and it was as if the earlier research had become redundant, as influencers could talk directly to consumers.[195] However, more recent research, with more fine-grained data, reinforced the impression that influence and impact are subject to the two-step-hypothesis. To wit, this model "still had explanatory power in online public forums. Opinion leaders were found to be influentials but not content creators".[196]

In a similar vein, it was also found that some influencers – including celebrities – could perform this role. However, the overall finding is that findings of "the 1955 two-step flow model are still valid". Thus, "while direct one-step flows and more complex network flows are also present . . . it is no contradiction that social media participants mainly refer to intermediating amplifiers of communicated messages (39 percent of the mentions from participants go through this two-step communication flow)".[197]

The task, therefore, is not merely to use social neuroscience to influence behaviour. Rather, the task is to identify opinion leaders, and to test their responses to information on issues related to hate and various phobias in a neuroscientific setting, which is to say, using fMRI scans or similar techniques.

The evidence is clear with (neuro)scientific research. Objective information works. We have no time to lose. As antisemitism is becoming tragically more prevalent, public information campaigns work to combat it. There is no time to lose.

So, where does this leave us? One official study was rather positive. It stated:

> Neuroscience has the potential to make important contributions to education. These potential contributions are of at least three kinds: novel under about biological and environmental processes determining learning; the identification of early neural markers for educational risk; and neural methods for evaluating different teaching methods for evaluating different teaching approaches, remediation packages or educational debates.[198]

That report was not, of course, the only one to recognise that social neuroscience has an important role to play in education. But although there is a recognition that "knowledge of how the brain learns could, and will, have a great impact on education", the "could" of this sentence has not been matched by the "will". To date, the use of social neuroscience remains an untapped source. Using social neuroscience can help home in on messages in a way that focus groups and expert opinion cannot.

This is necessary. Humans are not the only species capable of group-based cruelty towards “the other”. It is something we see in animals such as ants and chimpanzees. But unlike these other social animals, we are capable of being influenced by infomercials and adverts.

Social neuroscience has identified areas of the brain that are involved when we subconsciously show racist responses. And we know what happens. However, we also know from similar fMRI studies that we are not hardwired to be xenophobic. When people live with and associate with people of a different background or race, they become more tolerant.

But we do not have time to wait for people to be tolerant. So can we do something else? In fact, we can; there are studies that – through testing under the brain scanners – can home in on messages. When combined with the knowledge of how influencing works, we are in a position to truly harvest the insights of social neuroscience for good purposes.

In the words of Liya Yu, one of the pioneers of this approach, the perspective of social neuroscience:

> does not promise a complete or definitive explanatory framework about why and how exclusion and dehumanisation takes place or how it can be overcome. What it does set out from a viewpoint of political strategy, despite all these caveats, is to offer a neurobiologically inclusionary way to pitch the social contract to those whom we find hardest to convince at a time where there seems very little that opposed groups in our fractured liberal democracies have in common.[199]

Social neuroscience is not a panacea, but it is an approach that has proved to help us understand what we really think, and that can help us become better and more tolerant of each other. We cannot afford not to use it.

Chapter 8
The Social Neuroscience of Listening

"We are not what we know but what we are willing to learn". Mary Catherine Bateson (1939–2021), the famous anthropologist, said. Her motto was meant to convey her tolerance and openness to other cultures, and her conviction was that the essence of humanity is a willingness to listen.

This daughter of the ethnographer power couple, Margaret Mead and Gregory Bateson, grew up in an enlightened New York household where openness to other voices – preferably in their native tongues – was the order of the day (Mary herself was a polyglot and spoke at least ten foreign languages). Pithy though it was, her strapline was not unique. Others, too, have expressed the same sentiment – and the same philosophy of life. The Dalai Lama, to name one, has remarked, "when you talk you are only repeating what you already know, when you listen you learn something new".

Nothing, it seems, could be further from the adversarial – occasionally cutthroat – attitude that characterises politics today. The openness and acceptance of others that lie at the heart of these quotes seem to be the polar opposite – the antithesis, if you like – of the political debates we encounter on "X" and other, not always, "social" media.

The controversial social and legal theorist Carl Schmitt, who wrote in the 1920s, remarked that "we contrast good and bad in ethics, beautiful and ugly in aesthetics", but that the "specific juxtaposition to which all political actions and attitudes can be reduced is that between friend and enemy".[200] In the light of such definitions, it is tempting to conclude that openness and tolerance, and ultimately respect for other people, are incompatible with politics: that this is just an adversarial game of us-versus-them.

But there is reason to be cautious and not get carried away. Certainly, the shorthand of friend-versus-enemy is neat and diabolically elegant. But that does not make it right. Schmitt openly supported the dictatorship, and even joined the ranks of the tyrants after 1933.

Maybe today Schmitt's juxtaposition contains a kernel of truth even in democracies. But we should not be bowled over backwards by neat definitions. Eloquence does not establish a fact. The friend-enemy dichotomy was conceived in the dying days of the Weimar Republic at a time when enmity was the order of the day and where angry mobs clashed in the streets. That this definition chimes with what we are witnessing today is a cause for concern. It is a worrying indication of just how far we have drifted from the ideals of democratic governance

 | https://doi.org/10.1515/9783111616506-009

espoused by those who defended what Abraham Lincoln famously described as "government of the people, by the people, for the people".[201]

Certainly, there are camps, parties – and what used to be called "fractions"[202] – in places where the voters are the ultimate masters. But politics in democracies is so much more than adversarial. We know this in our heart of hearts. Yes, cynics may contend that those who speak of "the common good" are romantic, and possibly even naïve. This objection – rather conveniently – overlooks that many democratic societies have written this common goal in their names, the Commonwealth of Virginia, for example, and the Commonwealth of Australia. In these cases, it is explicit that we are not enemies, but in this together. That this is so is not just a quirk of English-speaking countries. The Swedish word for society, *Samhället*, literally translates to "that which holds us together". And *Samfund*, the Danish word for the same, is etymologically "that which we have discovered together". This has something to do with why we became the most powerful species on the Earth.

So why? What makes us so unique? It's all to do with evolution, in some way or an other. When early humans evolved more cranial space, it allowed for more space for the thinking parts because the spine, gradually and over millions of years, slid from the back to under the head. All this meant that we suddenly had room for the part of the brain that deals with executive functions, and we became a species that can "plan and delay gratification".[203] We have evidence of this from 23,000 years ago when humans developed fish traps and elaborate harpoons.[204] Termites have evolved snouts, chimpanzees with a relatively large prefrontal cortex have tools – if rudimentary and primitive ones at that – and we have civil engineering.

But we have something that other species do not have. Before I reveal what it is, let's keep up the suspense and ask another question. Here it is. Can't other primates make sounds? Yes, of course they can. Dogs bark and whales can sing. And before you object, yes, chimpanzees can make vocal noises, some of which show that our nearest relative in the animal kingdom has a kind of language.[205] But no. At best, other primates can merely point to things or express displeasure. All are very interesting to the zoologist, and even impressive to the layperson, but ultimately they do not begin to compare with humans.

"Neanderthal thinking". This is how a former US President described the policies of two governors of the opposing party.[206] It was not meant as a compliment. There are many myths about the abilities and intelligence of our close evolutionary cousins. Many of these are not true. In fact, the Neanderthals had larger brains than we do.[207] Size alone does not determine intelligence. Larger bodies require more brains to control the larger muscle mass. But overall, evolutionary biologists say, "our brain size is related to our needs to socialize".[208] But in one respect, Homo sapiens had an edge. Yes, our brains might have been smaller, and we might have been less intelligent. But we did have an edge. We could talk. Neanderthals did not have vocal cords that were as developed to the degree that we have.[209]

It was because we had the ability to complain, to listen and, hence, to improve things that we got an evolutionary edge. In some ways, this ability is part and parcel of the argument for democracy. Democratic countries are those where there is a plurality of ideas, and they are successful because our abilities to speak, and crucially, to listen give us an edge. In a way, you could say we are neurologically hardwired to be democratic.

This is where neuropolitics once more comes in. A simple fMRI scan of the human brain reveals that we have exceptionally developed areas for speech and listening, and moreover, that we can learn by exchanging views in a free and open discussion.

We have already looked at the amygdala, and the reader could be excused for thinking that we are but primitive beings who are visceral and angry. But, of course, our brains are more than that. An fMRI scan of the brain, when it is exposed to a simple political argument on economic policy, will show that the dorsolateral frontal cortex – the part associated, among other things, with listening, speaking and reasoning – will flare up. A person might sometimes be driven by amygdala responses. But this same person can also make a rational and considered argument. We humans all have the capacity to use the powers with which we have been endowed by evolution. When we do so, we not only solve problems in society but also engage our brains, which makes us less likely to develop degenerative conditions like Alzheimer's and Parkinson's.

We have a choice to make. So the evolution of the speech centres gave sapiens the brain power to cooperate, and combined with the vocal cords, the capacity to exchange views and learn from each other. In a sense, the rest is history. The history that we are about to tell, the story of the listening brain, the one capable of engaging in *Bouleusis*.

The most important part of the first element in the development of the democratic brain is the ability to engage in conversation. This ability stems from the give-and-take of communication. This capacity is due to two specific areas of the brain. These are called, respectively, the *Broca area* (associated with speech) and the *Wernicke area* (associate with listening).

That we have this ability to make decisions after we have listened, and we can, in turn, prompt others to make choices, is because we have a listening or, if you like, democratic brain. Discussion is a two-way street; it is talking as much as listening. “At the heart of a strong democracy is talk”, wrote the American writer and scholar Benjamin Barber.[210] So, the two people in the scan are not engaging in a perfect debate. The one on the right is less likely to learn from the person on the left and vice versa. But at least they are engaging.

The essence of this briefest of summaries of the language centres in our brains shows what happens when we engage in discussion. We do not – for rather obvious reasons – have brain scans of the Athenian males who were gathered to "take counsel" in the *Boule* – the legislative assembly – over 2,000 years ago. But if we did, it is a fair bet that we would get images akin to the ones shown above.

Why is all of this so important? Mainly because other species do not have this capacity. We still have parts of the brain that we share with other animals. We have the fight-and-flight part that allows us to react with vigour and rage when this is necessary – and occasionally when it isn't.

What is crucial is that our whole evolution as an *animal socialis* – a social being – hinges on the unique ability to communicate through language.[211] What the scan shows and what our knowledge of neuroscience teaches us is that we have been successful because we have these capabilities – this knack for learning through listening. If we do not use this ability, if we simply act by instinct, we are certainly not fulfilling our evolutionary potential. And who knows, perhaps we might even go backwards on the evolutionary ladder.

We are not merely created for rage and impulse, nor for compassion and sympathy. We are able to use our capacity for communication to improve our condition and to learn from it. Of course, this ability would be of little use if we did not have other higher faculties as well. Solving problems together, "taking counsel" is useful only because we can put that knowledge to good use through all the other capabilities we have, thanks to other parts of the brain.

We have a democratic brain because this form of government, at its heart, is based *on bouleúō* – or, as we may translate it, "deliberative listening".

We have the capacity to listen and learn. We aren't, yet we're like, animals. Our decisions are – or ought to be – made after we have weighed up the facts, the pros and the cons. That we have evolved societies, that we have moved beyond just living a hand-to-mouth existence on the savannah is because we have utilised this listening brain. But to continue to do so, we need to exercise caution lest we fall backwards into anger and react instinctively rather than through reflection. We need to utilise and exercise the higher cortex that brought us here, and not always fall back on a limbic system that is designed only to be used in case of emergency. And to do so means, above all, to engage in *Bouleusis.*

Democracy – the way it was described by the Greek authors – was rather practical. It was an exercise in problem-solving. The aim was not merely to win support for our ideas and get others to vote for our pet projects. The Greeks did not have ideologies. There might have been differences, but in matters of public policy, it was a matter of finding solutions. The process, as it was spelled out by Aristotle, was as follows: "[citizens] ask how a policy can be accomplished by what means, and by what means that means can itself be achieved. They do so until they reach the first link in the chain of causes, which is the last in the order of discovery. *Bouleusis* as described is thus pursuing an investigation."[212]

All too often, political debates at this time of hyperpolarisation start with the answer; with an ideologically coloured conclusion, be that less immigration, lower taxation or higher spending. This is not the best way to engage our brains. There is no investigation and no engagement with other views. We are what we know – and we are not willing to learn.

If we are to fully fulfil our cerebral potential, we need to practise a different kind of politics, one that looks for solutions to established problems. When Aristotle wrote about the Greek city-state, he wrote that we deliberated about things "when we are more uncertain about them".[213]

To solve political problems, we need to focus much more on implementation and less on ideology. This fundamentally means that we must take our fellow beings seriously. To take this attitude, we need to fundamentally revise how we understand and engage in political debates. We have to go beyond the us-versus-them and towards a being-in-this-together approach.

That certain institutions can facilitate this is a topic well worth exploring at length. But suffice it to say that the democratic brain needs to focus if it is to live up to its full potential.

Sometimes it has been said that "Democracy is a way of life". Tomáš Masaryk (1850–1937), a scholar-politician who became the first president of Czechoslovakia, also defined this system of government as "discussion". "But the real discussion is possible only if people trust each other and if they are trying fairly to find the truth. Democracy is a conversation among equals."[214] Life is much easier if we simply focus on the ones we like or dislike. But it becomes more difficult if we actually have to rack our brains for practical solutions. That politics is problem-solving is something that we often tend to forget. Yet, throughout the ages, those who have written about the art and science of governing a country from a democratic point of view have stressed that this system requires humbleness and a willingness to learn.

Even your fiercest ideological foe has evolved a brain just like yours. They, too, are a product of 5 million plus years of evolutionary history, over the course of which you both – we all – became the most sophisticated species that we know. And this has implications for the way we talk to fellow citizens and treat one an other.

Whichever political team you root for, and whichever politicians you find abhorrent or the opposite, as citizens in a democratic society, we have the opportunity, indeed, the obligation, to contribute to practical solutions. We have a brain that is designed to solve problems through discussion. We do injustice to ourselves if we do not use it.

Note that he, too, saw political decision-making as a journey of discovery and as part of a collective investigation. His argument for democracy was practical: based on the superior outcomes of allowing people to find solutions. This is still a valid argument. Spinoza, no doubt, would be delighted to hear that there are other arguments for using our brains. We are hardwired to think democratically. We evolved our brains to create societies, arts and poetry because we have the ability to speak, listen and learn.

But there is an aspect of this process that we have not looked at so far, another reason why we must encourage *bouleúō* – deliberative listening – as we not only solve problems when we engage in this process of taking counsel.

Nor is this process solely to be cherished because it re-establishes the equal worth of others with the same brain as ours – though that is important too. The process of engaging our democratic brain is also desirable because it makes us cleverer – and even healthier. For our brains – like our muscles – work best when they are exercised. The more we train the brain, the more neurological pathways we keep open, and the healthier we become. When we are engaging our brain in the process of democratic learning, we stay healthy.

So where does this chapter leave us? The answer is simple. If we are to fulfil our brain's potential, we need to change the way we do politics away from hate speech and towards the ideal of *Bouleusis*.

Chapter 9
A Detour into Body and Soul

To write about neuropolitics is likely to throw up philosophical thoughts of all sorts, at least for me. It was the same with my paternal grandfather. He was excited to begin his studies in philosophy at the University of Copenhagen in 1924. He had read about Kant, Kierkegaard and Plato, and now it was the real deal. He was surprised when the professor began talking about anatomy and biology. The distinguished professor was Jørgen Jørgensen – a self-proclaimed logical positivist, who took the view that all philosophical issues should be reduced to measurable science without any resort to medieval or other metaphysics. He told his audience of newcomers to the university that psychology could be – indeed, ought to be! – reduced to biology.

My grandfather was shocked, and yet – so he later recalled to me – summoned the courage to ask the distinguished professor a question,

"Sir, you have spoken eloquently and with great learning about the human body. But you are yet to mention the soul. How is that and where does that fit in?"

The professor – an imposing figure with a bushy Karl Marx-like beard (he was also a member of the Communist Party) – gave my grandfather a condescending look, sighed and answered,

"Young man, as you will be aware, anatomists have dissected human bodies for well over 2000 years. At no point during this time have they found the so-called soul. So, common sense clearly tells us that the soul does not exist!"

My grandfather – in his 18-year-old freshman incarnation straight from the country-side – shot back,

"But, Sir, have they found common sense?"

He later told me, with barely hidden pride, that the professor had been left speechless and had taken no further questions. My grandfather changed his major to theology. Jørgen Jørgensen is largely forgotten. The once-so-mighty man does not even have a Wikipedia page. *Sic transit gloria mundi?*

Not exactly, for much as we may – and ought to – cheer those who challenge authority, the now-forgotten professor's view of the world is one largely shared by philosophers and neuroscientists who study the brain. There has been a lot of water under the proverbial bridges since then. Let's take a step back and put this into philosophical and historical perspective.[215]

For starters, my grandfather was rather doctrinaire. His witty response to the philosophy professor is neat, not least because it is a case of the underdog show-

 | https://doi.org/10.1515/9783111616506-010

ing up a cocky superior. But, at other times, he, too, could show the same inflexibility as Professor Jørgensen.

"No, that Darwin guy was wrong. God created man. That is how great God is!", he told me with the same firmness with which he had rebuked the professor. I was 6 years old at the time and did not have the eloquence and wit to respond, so I just ran to my mother, who calmed me that, Grandpa has many ideas. But that doesn't mean he was right, of course. This is not to bore you with stories from my childhood. But only to illustrate that the issue of the soul, and more generally science and religion often plays a role in discussions about this.

Many books have been written about this topic, and literally by the greatest minds ever to have lived, so I can merely scratch the surface here, and give you the briefest of overviews about the matter.

Aristotle was called a common-sense philosopher. He was interested in dissecting things – like the anatomists the professor cited. He famously founded the discipline of biology (alongside that of psychology, by the way), which was focused on what he could observe and measure. He believed that our feelings resided in our heart (which is why we associate this organ with feelings today), and that the brain was just a mechanism for cooling down the system. Aristotle did not believe that there was life after death, as he did not think we had a soul that was independent of our body. It was not an unusual idea at the time.

In fact, it is rather interesting to see how materialist – or monist (to use a technical expression) – many thinkers were. Take Hippocrates. He is, by common consent, the father of the science of medicine. He lived at a time when people would seek the advice of the oracle in Delphi and believe in Hades after death. Yet he was also of the view that we were basically just biology. "Men [and presumably women and non-binary] ought to know that from the brain, and the brain only, arise our pleasures, joys, laughter and jests, as well as our sorrows, pains, griefs and tears."[216]

Interestingly, the same view was taken in the Old Testament. The ancient Israelites did not believe in an immaterial soul. In fact, historically speaking, one of the challenges that the High Priests in the New Testament faced from Jesus Christ was that the self-proclaimed "Son of God" preached that we do have a soul and an afterlife, even when our brains have ceased to work.[217]

Social neuroscience deals with an issue that has exercised minds for millennia, but in different ways. Those interested in politics – and philosophy and theology – have always been puzzled by what drives us and why we make decisions. This pondering led to the birth of philosophy. Over 2,000 years ago, the philosopher Plato said that our minds are divided into reason and anger when we feel "left behind". Thus, democracies broke down because the citizens demanded ever more recognition and rose up because they perceived they were not given – what they themselves considered to be – their due respect. Under these circumstances, they would often, puzzlingly, undercut their own freedoms by electing an autocrat who claimed to speak on their behalf. Angry that they have been left out, the political system would become polarised, and Plato wrote, "hence arise impeachments, prosecutions, and trials, directed by each party against the other", and before long the people will "select a special champion of their cause, whom they maintain and exalt to greatness". All of this had to do with *Thymos*. When a man or a woman feels that someone "has been unjust to him [or her]", the "spirit within them" starts "boiling" and she or he will be "fighting for what this individual believes to be just".[218]

To write about the brain and decisions is likely to open a hornet's nest of controversy. In the history of philosophy and science, there has always been an argument about the ontological status of our mind.

Some philosophers, most notably René Descartes, famously claimed that we were a mixture of body and soul – respectively, *res extensa* and *res cogitans*.[219]

For philosophers, the situation was even more pronounced. While Benedict Spinoza was sympathetic towards a materialistic interpretation, in his *Ethics*, he was convinced that "mind and body are one and the same". He also acknowledged that – at least at the time – "no one knows how or by what means the mind moves the body".[220]

Locke's famous *Essay Concerning Human Understanding* struck an even more downcast prediction as to what we can know about the neurobiological side of the mind, writing that "we have the ideas of matter and thinking, but possibly shall never be able to know whether any mere material thinks or no".[221]

While there were thinkers in subsequent centuries who espoused a muscular materialism, it was not until the last decade of the twentieth century that we were able to (indirectly) associate brain activity with thoughts and tasks. Thanks to fMRI scans, we can see what goes on in our heads when we think about politics.

Does this all mean that the debate has been won by materialists, that my grandfather's professor was right? Most twentieth-century philosophers would probably think so. Gilbert Ryle, an Oxford don and the author of The *Concept of Mind*, and a man with an incisive turn of phrase who referred to Descartes' concept of the soul as a "ghost in the machine", wrote:

> With the doubtful exceptions of idiots and infants in arms every human being has both a body and a mind. Some would prefer to say that every human being is both a body and a mind. His body and his mind are ordinarily harnessed together, but after the death of the body his mind may continue to exist and function. Human bodies are in space and are subject to the mechanical laws which govern all other bodies in space. Bodily processes and states can be inspected by external observers. So a man's bodily life is as much a public

> affair as are the lives of animals and reptiles and even as the careers of trees, crystals and planets. But minds are not in space, nor are their operations subject to mechanical laws.[222]

It is these mechanical laws that we can see in operation in fNIRS and fMRI scans. I used to be terrified by the prospect that I am just a walking, talking amalgam of chemical processes, or just a flesh-and-blood computer that would cease to think once my life was over. As I have grown older, and as I am approaching my end, I have, on balance, grown more relaxed about this. Perhaps I have realised that the greatest sin in life is that of a soul afraid of dying, one that forgets to live. Perhaps we are but chemical processes? Or perhaps not. Or perhaps some – especially those who subscribe to various interpretations of quantum mechanics. Albert Einstein famously observed that matter can be turned into energy, and perhaps this immaterial force is the thing in us that lives on. Certainly, while many neuroscientists are materialists, in the sense that Gilbert Ryle was, quantum physicists have taken a more spiritualist approach. Max Planck, for one, believed:

> All matter originates and exists only by virtue of a force which brings the particle of an atom to vibration and holds this most minute solar system of the atom together. We must assume behind this force the existence of a conscious and intelligent mind. This mind is the matrix of all matter.[223]

Somehow this makes me feel relieved.

Chapter 10
Bringing It All Back Home

The second you read this sentence, your brain is exposed to 11 million bits of information.[224] But only fifty of these are processed. Yes, the brain is rather remarkable. What you process will depend very much on who you are. We are not alike.

Oxley et al. wrote:

> Although political views have been thought to arise largely from individuals' experiences, recent research suggests that they may have a biological basis. We present evidence that variations in political attitudes correlate with physiological traits. In a group of 46 adult participants with strong political beliefs, individuals with measurably lower physical sensitivities to sudden noises and threatening visual images were more likely to support foreign aid, liberal immigration policies, pacifism, and gun control, whereas individuals displaying measurably higher physiological reactions to those same stimuli were more likely to favor defense spending, capital punishment, patriotism, and the Iraq War. Thus, the degree to which individuals are physiologically responsive to threat appears to indicate the degree to which they advocate policies that protect the existing social structure from both external (outgroup) and internal (norm-violator) threats.[225]

As this book has shown, we have politics on our minds. Or, perhaps, more accurately, we have politics in many parts of the *cerebrum* (the Latin name for said organ).

But until recently, political scientists – and, indeed, even psychologists and philosophers – failed to use neuropolitics when analysing political and policy issues. Politics – insofar as it was measured – was understood through the prism of opinion polling and focus groups, and in some cases through the writings of old masters and political philosophers. The same was true for disciplines such as law and business studies. We have touched upon the latter two disciplines in this book, but our focus has been on politics. So, I will continue with that.

In many ways, it was odd that political scientists did not go back to the basics of decision-making and ask what causes us to make choices. Psychology would have been the clear choice for political scientists.

I mean, after all, it is a behavioural science that deals with the motives for choosing one party rather than another. Yet, to use psychology, you need to build on solid foundations. And these were not forthcoming. In academic psychology, Freud and his followers hypothesised the existence of a subconscious *id* in constant battle with the *superego*, but never even sought to locate this in the brain,[226] and even more so, the aptly named behavioural psychologists looked at patterns

 | https://doi.org/10.1515/9783111616506-011

of behaviour and treated the mind as a "black box", that is to say, something that we do not understand and can't get inside.[227]

This didn't change much when political science turned towards rational-choice analysis and institutionalism in the 1980s. These were theories that basically said that voters think like consumers and vote for parties that give them the greatest economic benefits.

It slightly puzzled me as a newcomer to the science of politics. Having originally started my academic journey in neuroscience, I was so obsessed with politics (and disappointed with brain science) that I transferred to Politics (as this academic subject is called at Oxford) and eventually gained a doctorate in this discipline.

However, I was surprised to find that no references at all were made to biology in my new discipline. While I was fascinated by the rigour of the sophisticated models of electoral behaviour, and even used them in my own research to forecast the outcomes of referendums, such as the "Brexit vote",[228] I was never fully convinced by the claimed advances of fancy statistical models that seemed to forecast everything. Still, I was happy to use them and published articles that sought to explain such matters as terrorism and voting behaviour using the narrow definition of human behaviour used by economists.

At the risk of providing a bit too much autobiography, I went on to analyse terrorism using this framework and concluded that political violence is the result of a weighing-up of the costs and benefits of engaging in democratic politics or, alternatively, of forcing yourself into the political system by, so to speak, blowing its door off its hinges.[229] My contention was that the more inclusive the political system (e.g. the more it allows minorities to participate through "consensus" institutions like proportional representation), the less likely we were to experience political violence.

Yet when I lectured on the subject, people pointed out that the argument was simplistic and that my "grievance theory" (the one just cited) was perhaps too neat, a bit too abstract and just plain simplistic. My argument, as admirably summed up by a prominent critic, was that "political violence occurs when societal grievances do not find political expression and accommodation". However, the same critic found that I did not adequately demonstrate or prove an empirical relationship between consensus democracy and terrorism.[230] At the time, I stubbornly held to my position in public, but I had a lingering doubt about it in private and quietly conceded the point. It is, I reflected, one thing to predict something mathematically, or even find a correlation; it is something entirely different to show a motive and to present a rounded theory.

What I personally found interesting – and, secretly found mildly disturbing – was that the rational choice models work only part of the time. And perhaps, above all, that the "wildly inaccurate descriptive representations of reality" – to quote Friedman – were not, and often could not be, justified by accurate predictions. Behaviourally we are occasionally rational – and then, sometimes – we lose our proverbial marbles and act out of anger or on instinct. This line of reasoning was ultimately bordering on being banal, like the statement "it rains except when it doesn't".

So, for this reason, I gradually and slowly began to return to neuroscience. This discipline, which I had followed only sporadically, had not stood still.

What I wanted to know was why and when we act rationally, and why we sometimes do the opposite, that is, not just answering a banal statement like, "Birds either fly or they don't", but using the same metaphor to explain what prompts them to take flight, i.e. to identify the cause of them flying off. Hence, I figured that a truly new theory would be one that distinguished between (and explained) when we make a rational decision and when we do not.

Such distinctions, I was aware, had been proposed before in the history of political philosophy. For example, in his *Republic* (and later in *Phaedros*), Plato introduced a tripartite division of the soul. In his reading, it consisted of *Thymos* (the emotional element) and *epithumia* (appetite and generally bodily desires), and these were to be ruled over by *nous* (commonly, if somewhat inaccurately, translated as "intellect").[231] But things have moved on since Plato. And much as I admire and idolise the great Greek sage, I wanted to bring his thinking up to date, or rather to complement it through the recent advances in neuroscience.

My ambition was (and is) to see if we could somehow combine the approaches of philosophy and neuroscience and find a place for rational choice as a subset of one of the behaviours. The aim of this short book, then, is to put the Friedmanian rationality in its place: not to abandon it, as it is still a valuable approach. Rather, the aim is to find out where and when it can be used, and to understand the biological as well as the philosophical aspects of human behaviour. But overall, the ambition is to develop a new science of politics, a new paradigm that (in part at least) explains political behaviour through an understanding of the brain.

All this, I should add, is nothing new. Although that is true, few, if any, have combined neuropolitics with philosophy. Much as this may sound new to many readers, there are, in fact, several studies that look at the neurobiological bases of our political behaviour.[232] And not just new ones, I might add.

This little book, then, has not invented the study of politics through brain science and neurology. But then again, Thomas Hobbes did not invent the mechanistic view of the world; he merely applied this model to create a new synthesis. Likewise, David Hume did not invent Newtonian physics, but what the Scottish philosopher did was to “introduce the experimental Method of Reasoning into Moral Subjects”.[233]

This is an attempt to reintroduce neuroscientific methods into political philosophy and empirical political science. How, then, is this possible? The main answer to that is that we now have fMRI scans, which allow us indirectly to see what goes on in the mind when we are presented with different facts or images, or are performing different tasks.

One of the things that these developments and advances in neuroscience allow us to do is to put Hobbes, Spinoza, Aristotle and Plato in the fMRI scanner and see what goes on in our brains when we are exposed to extreme (and mundane) political statements.

As I was researching this, it seemed that others had already been thinking along the same lines. One writer noted: “naturally, there is no shortage of studies about the brain and its political inclinations. And it seems that liberals have [a] slightly larger anterior cingulate cortex (the part of the frontal cortex above the corpus callosum), while conservatives allegedly have an atrophied right amygdala.”[234] At a personal level, I was excited to see this. When I took up political science in the early 1990s, these methods had yet to be developed. They are now. And this has radical implications for the way we see and do political analysis. As it turned out, the reference to “no shortage of studies” is somewhat overcooked, and there is a relative paucity of studies – at least at the time of writing – that cover brain politics.

But all great things start with small beginnings; Rome was not built in a day, and so on. As already noted, this book is not the first one to use these approaches to study political attitudes and behaviours. And there is, despite the relative dearth of studies, already something to build on – just as there was something on which Hume could base his *Treatise*. In a recent review article (albeit one written in a slightly forbidding language), the authors sum up the advances in the following words, in a section that deserves to be quoted at length:

> The emerging interdisciplinary field of political neuroscience (or neuropolitics) is focused on understanding the neural mechanisms underlying political information processing and decision making. . . . This includes brain regions involved in affective and evaluative processing, such as the amygdala, insula, anterior cingulate, and orbitofrontal cortex, as well as regions involved in social cognition (e.g., medial prefrontal cortex [PFC]), decision making (e.g., dorsolateral PFC), and reward processing (e.g., ventral striatum). Existing research in political neuroscience has largely focused on understanding candidate evaluation, political participation, and ideological differences. . . . While the field is still relatively new, this work has begun to improve our understanding of how people engage in motivated reasoning about political candidates and elected officials and the extent to which these processes may be automatic versus relatively more controlled. Other work has focused on under-

> standing how brain differences are related to differences in political opinion, showing both structural and functional variation between political liberals and political conservatives.[235]

"There is room for words on subjects other than last words", wrote my one-time teacher, the late great philosopher Robert Nozick.[236] This book, in the same spirit, is anything but final. Rather, it is intended to be located among other conversations rather than as the last word on neuropolitics.

In the chapters above, the book has introduced a perspective that remains unknown and esoteric to many social scientists. In addition to providing a crash course in social neuroscience and, indeed, in the biology of the brain itself, I hope this book has brought together different strands of this new subfield in political science and neuroscience in a way that not only covers the different areas of research but also puts the endeavours of scholars into historical and philosophical context.

What we have found in this little book is that certain areas of the brain are activated when individuals are engaged in politics (see box below) and that there are differences between the brains of conservatives and liberals.

Brain Regions Activated in Political Thinking among Conservatives and Liberals

Mostly Conservatives
Amygdala (anger and fear)
Ventral striatum (reward processing)
Dorsolateral prefrontal cortex (decision-making and inhibition)
Orbitofrontal cortex (emotions, social behaviours)

Mostly Liberals
Insula (empathy and disgust)
Anterior cingulate cortex (impulse control and empathy)
Medial prefrontal cortex (social cognition)

As you will have seen by now, there has been an explosion of research into neuropolitics after new developments in the study of neuroscience that were pioneered in the 1990s.

While earlier, studies of the brain and political attitudes relied on studies of individuals with injuries,[237] technological advances such as fMRI scans enabled neuroscientists to study what happened inside people's heads when they were engaged in various activities.[238] Around the turn of the millennium, these studies began to take off in the fields of politics, law and economics.[239]

But some findings may be more controversial. In political science, you need to be fair-minded. We – and I think I speak for most colleagues – are acutely aware that we can easily be accused of bias. This sometimes means that we go to absurd degrees to present even outrageous characters in neutral language. This is understandable. We are commentators, not actors in the game.

But there is a risk that a *wertfrei* science becomes bland. And sometimes it is important not to shy away from statements for fear that they are controversial. Political science needs to be objective and not politicised. But what if the insights reveal differences between the two sides of politics that paint one side in a better light? Ought we not to say so for fear of being political?

Whatever you think the answer to these questions is, the fact (sic!) remains that one side of the political spectrum is more driven by emotion than the other. The insights of neuroscience were summed up in an article in *Scientific American*, which stated, "On the whole, the research shows, conservatives desire more security, predictability and authority than liberals do, and liberals are more comfortable with novelty, nuance, and complexity". That is, perhaps, uncontroversial. But the next sentence was not: "the volume of grey matter, or neural cell bodies making up the anterior cingulate cortex, an area that helps detect errors and resolve conflicts, tends to be larger in liberals. And the amygdala, which is important for regulating emotions and evaluating threats, is larger in conservatives."[240]

The stories I have told in the chapters above show that Liberals generally use the more sophisticated parts of the brain, whereas some on the radical right resort to amygdala responses, which would seem to suggest that the former are more likely to engage in rational debate than the latter. That might be drawing too strong a conclusion. However, we should not forget that the research also shows that conservative voters (and those who, according to Implicit Association Tests, are on the right) tend to have more activated dorsolateral prefrontal cortices – an area that is associated with caution but also with economic thinking. So, it is not all bad for those on the right.

Those on the left may not be the only ones to make use of the insula, but it is not far from being the case. Neuropolitically speaking, liberals are kinder and more likely to use nuanced arguments – whereas conservatives are more prone to rely on more evolutionarily primitive parts of the brain. Those on the right, by contrast, may be sceptical and cautious, which is a characteristic that has served us well through evolution. Conversely, having empathy has meant that we care for the weak in a way that is unique in the animal kingdom. We need both aspects of the brain to progress further.

We are all the product of millions of years of biological evolution. We all have amygdala responses, and we all have the capacity to use the insula and the dorsolateral prefrontal cortex. We can all get angry, but we also all possess the ability to listen and discuss: in other words, to democratically deliberate over policy issues.

What neuropolitics shows is not just that there are subtle differences in the parts of the brain that are activated when we are prompted, but also that we – alone among species – are social problem-solvers. We are an adaptive species, one that learns from interaction with fellow human beings. And this brings us back to the apparent fact that we are hardwired to listen and learn from each other.

Democracy is discussion, and for that you need the ability to discuss and deliberate. What distinguishes us from other animals is the ability to do exactly this, and this gave us an edge in evolution. As a neuropsychologist has put it, "the ability to teach and learn through ways other than through example and imitation [was a] crucial marker of our success".[241]

Neuroscience can help us understand the reasons for our actions and our thoughts. Realising that we may be driven more by the amygdala than by activity in the frontal lobes, that we act on instinct, and that we do not use the parts of the brain that evolution bestowed upon us will hopefully make us stop and think (yes!). Maybe we, the Homo sapiens – the thinking human – will be embarrassed that we resort to hate and not to deliberation. And maybe, if we are poetic souls, we will agree with the Bard's wise words from *Macbeth*:

> "Raze out the written troubles of the brain".[242]

Endnotes

1 https://timesofmalta.com/article/matt-qvortrup-give-philosophy-sharing-foundation-lecture.1086748
2 Yu, L. (2022). *Vulnerable Minds: The Neuropolitics of Divided Societies.* New York: Columbia University Press.
3 Ludwig Wittgenstein (1953) *Philosophical Investigations.* Oxford: Blackwell, p. vii.
4 Zebarjadi, N., Adler, E., Kluge, A., Sams, M., & Levy, J. (2023). Ideological values are parametrically associated with empathy neural response to vicarious suffering. *Social Cognitive and Affective Neuroscience, 18*(1), p. 2
5 Kanai, R., Feilden, T., Firth, C., & Rees, G. (2011). Political orientations are correlated with brain structure in young adults. *Current biology, 21*(8), 677–680.
6 John T. Cacioppo & Gary G. Berntson (1992). Social psychological contributions to the decade of the brain: Doctrine of multilevel analysis. *American Psychologist*, 47(8), 1019–1028.
7 John, J., Kodama, T., & Siegel, J. M. (2014). Caffeine promotes glutamate and histamine release in the posterior hypothalamus. *American Journal of Physiology-Regulatory, Integrative and Comparative Physiology, 307*(6), R704–R710.
8 De Dreu, C. K., Greer, L. L., Van Kleef, G. A., Shalvi, S., & Handgraaf, M. J. (2011). Oxytocin promotes human ethnocentrism. *Proceedings of the National Academy of Sciences, 108*(4), 1262–1266.
9 Carter, C. S., & Porges, S. W. (2013). The biochemistry of love: An oxytocin hypothesis. Science & Society Series on Sex and Science. *EMBO reports, 14*(1), 12–16.
10 Kiser, D., Steemer S. B., Branchi, I., & Homberg, J. R. (2012). The reciprocal interaction between serotonin and social behaviour. *Neuroscience & Biobehavioral Reviews, 36*(2), 786–798, p. 786.
11 https://www.health.harvard.edu/mind-and-mood/serotonin-the-natural-mood-booster Accessed June 6, 2025.
12 Lembke, A. (2021). *Dopamine Nation: Finding Balance in the Age of Indulgence.* London: Penguin.
13 Berridge, K. C. (2007). The debate over dopamine's role in reward: The case for incentive salience. *Psychopharmacology, 191*, 391–431.
14 Leor Zmigrod (2025) *The Ideological Brain: The Radical Science of Susceptible Minds.* London: Penguin, p. 142.
15 Zmigrod, ibid.
16 Melville, H. (1851). *Moby Dick; or, The Whale.* New York: Harper and Brothers, Chapter 10.
17 As reported in Andrews, D. (2016) *Neuropsychology.* Abingdon: Routledge, p. 516.
18 Maguire, E. A., Gadian, D. G., Johnsrude, I. S., Good, C. D., Ashburner, J., Frackowiak, R. S., & Frith, C. D. (2000). Navigation-related structural change in the hippocampi of taxi drivers. *Proceedings of the National Academy of Sciences, 97*(8), 4398–4403, p. 4398.
19 Weir, B. (2011). A history of neurosurgery in Canada. *Canadian Journal of Neurological Sciences, 38*(2), 203–219. Born in Manchester in 1918, Dr Milner is still active at the age of 104 at the time of writing and a full professor at McGill University in Montreal.
20 Babaeeghazvini, P., Rueda-Delgado, L. M., Gooijers, J., Swinnen, S. P., & Daffertshofer, A. (2021). Brain structural and functional connectivity: A review of combined works of diffusion magnetic resonance imaging and electro-encephalography. *Frontiers in Human Neuroscience, 15*, 721206. See also: Honey, C. J., Thivierge, J. P., and Sporns, O. (2010). Can structure predict function in the human brain? *NeuroImage, 52*, 766–776.

 | https://doi.org/10.1515/9783111616506-012

21 Luria, A. R. (1973). *The Working Brain: An Introduction to Neuropsychology*. London: Harmondsworth.
22 Andrews, *Neuropsychology*, p. 19.
23 Luria, *The Working Brain*, p. 89.
24 Takahashi, H., Kato, M., Matsuura, M., Mobbs, D., Suhara, T., & Okubo, Y. (2009). When your gain is my pain and your pain is my gain: Neural correlates of envy and schadenfreude. *Science, 323*(5916), 937–939. doi:10.1126/science.1165604
25 Bachnik, J. M. (2019). Uchi/soto: Authority and intimacy, hierarchy and solidarity in Japan. In Bachnik, J. M., & Quinn Jr., C. J. (Eds.). (2019), *Situated Meaning: Inside and Outside in Japanese Self, Society, and Language* (Vol. 5263). Princeton, NJ: Princeton University Press, pp. 223–243.
26 In statistical terms the correlation was $R = .65$ which is an unusually high correlation. This one is statistically significant at $p < 0.02$. Takahashi, H. et al., When your pain is my gain, p. 938.
27 Kringelbach, M. L. (2005). The human orbitofrontal cortex: Linking reward to hedonic experience. *Nature Reviews Neuroscience, 6*(9), 691–702.
28 Miyazaki, K., Miyazaki, K. W., Yamanaka, A., Tokuda, T., Tanaka, K. F., & Doya, K. (2018). Reward probability and timing uncertainty alter the effect of dorsal raphe serotonin neurons on patience. *Nature Communications, 9*(1), 2048.
29 Hull, E. M., Muschamp, J. W., & Sato, S. (2004). Dopamine and serotonin: Influences on male sexual behavior. *Physiology & Behavior, 83*(2), 291–307.
30 Gallucci, A., Riva, P., Lauro, L. J. R., & Bushman, B. J. (2020). Stimulating the ventrolateral prefrontal cortex (VLPFC) modulates frustration-induced aggression: A tDCS experiment. *Brain Stimulation, 13*(2), 302–309.
31 Knutson K., Wood, J., Spampinato, M., & Grafman, J. (2006) Politics on the brain: An fMRI Investigation. *Social Neuroscience, 1*(1), 25–40.
32 Leong, Y. C., Chen, J., Willer, R., & Zaki, J. (2020). Conservative and liberal attitudes drive polarized neural responses to political content. *Proceedings of the National Academy of Sciences, 117*-(44), 27731–27739, p. 27735.
33 de Bruin, D., van Baar, J. M., Rodríguez, P. L., & FeldmanHall, O. (2023). Shared neural representations and temporal segmentation of political content predict ideological similarity. *Science Advances, 9*(5), eabq5920.
34 Havel, V. [1978] (2009). *The Power of the Powerless Citizens Against the State in Central-Eastern Europe*. London: Routledge, p. 7.
35 Cole, G. D. H. (1935). London: Gollancz, p. 35.
36 Frank, T. (2004). *What's the Matter with Kansas?* New York: Metropolitan Books, p. 67.
37 Gabay, A. S., Radua, J., Kempton, M. J., & Mehta, M. A. (2014). The Ultimatum Game and the brain: A meta-analysis of neuroimaging studies. *Neuroscience & Biobehavioral Reviews, 47*, 549–558.
38 Hosokawa, T., Kennerley, S. W., Sloan, J., & Wallis, J. D. (2013). Single-neuron mechanisms underlying cost-benefit analysis in frontal cortex. *Journal of Neuroscience, 33*(44), 17385–17397.
39 The Rt Hon. Anne-Marie Trevelyan, personal communication, January 15, 2025.
40 Rawnsley, A. (2001). *Servants of the People: The Inside Story of New Labour*. Penguin UK, p. 213.
41 Jabbi, M., Bastiaansen, J., & Keysers, C. (2008). A common anterior insula representation of disgust observation, experience and imagination shows divergent functional connectivity pathways. *PLoS One, 3*(8), Article ID e2939.
42 Mendez, M. F. (2017). A neurology of the conservative-liberal dimension of political ideology. *The Journal of Neuropsychiatry and Clinical Neurosciences, 29*(2), 86–94, p. 89.

43 Eddy, C. M. (2016). The junction between self and other? Temporo-parietal dysfunction in neuropsychiatry. *Neuropsychologia, 89*, 465–477.
44 Tusche, A., Kahnt, T., Wisniewski, D., & Haynes, J. D. (2013). Automatic processing of political preferences in the human brain. *Neuroimage, 72*, 174–182.
45 Eddy, C. M. (2016). The junction between self and other? Temporo-parietal dysfunction in neuropsychiatry. *Neuropsychologia, 89*, 465–477.
46 Zebarjadi, N., Kluge, A., Adler, E., & Levy, J. (2024). New vistas for the relationship between empathy and political ideology. *eNeuro, 11*(11), p. 10.
47 Yun, J. H., Kim, Y., & Lee, E. J. (2022). ERP study of liberals' and conservatives' moral reasoning processes: Evidence from South Korea. *Journal of Business Ethics, 176*(4), 723–739.
48 Ogawa, A., Asano, S., Osada, T., Tanaka, M., Tochigi, R., Kamagata, K., . . . & Konishi, S. (2023). Role of right temporoparietal junction for counterfactual evaluation of partner's decision in ultimatum game. *Cerebral Cortex, 33*(6), 2947–2957.
49 https://tomlehrersongs.com/wp-content/uploads/2018/12/the-folk-song-army.pdf
50 Johnson, P. (2024). Owning the libs: The contemporary politics of envy. *Theory & Event, 27*(2), 233–257.
51 Aristotle *Rhetoric*, Book II, Part 10.
52 Cairns, D. L. (2019). The politics of envy: Envy and equality in ancient Greece. In D. Konstan (Ed.), *Envy, Spite and Jealousy: The Rivalrous Emotions in Ancient* (pp. 235–52). Edinburgh University Press.
53 Thatcher, M. (1974, September 22). Britain Can Win, *News of the World.*
54 Fliessbach, K., Weber, B., Trautner, P., Dohmen, T., Sunde, U., Elger, C. E., & Falk, A. (2007). Social comparison affects reward-related brain activity in the human ventral striatum. *Science, 318*(5854), 1305–1308.
55 di Pellegrino, G, Fadiga, L., Fogassi, L., Gallese, V., & Rizzolatti G. (1992). Understanding motor events: A neurophysiological study. *Experimental Brain Research, 91*(1), 176–180.
56 Lisovenko, A., Kriukova, M., Absalyamova, L., Chukhrii, I., Korchakova, N., & Androsovych, K. (2022). Neuropsychological fundamentals of envy. *BRAIN. Broad Research in Artificial Intelligence and Neuroscience, 13*(1), 158–172, at p. 158.
57 Lisovenko, A., et al. Neuropsychological Fundamentals of Envy, p. 168.
58 Cipolotti, L., Mole, J., Ruffle, J. K., Nelson, A., Gray, R., & Nachev, P. (2025). Cognitive control & the anterior cingulate cortex: Necessity & coherence. *Cortex*, 182, 87–99.
59 Locke, J. (1689). *An Essay Concerning Human Understanding*, I.1.8, N: 47.
60 Seeger, P. (1966). *Dangerous Songs*. Columbia Records.
61 Gallant, Jack, L., et al. (2011). Reconstructing visual experiences from brain activity evoked by natural movies. *Current Biology, 21*(19), 1641–1646.
62 Waugh, R. (2011, October 28). Brain scanner 'reads' people's dreams – accurately enough to see what they are dreaming about. *The Daily Mail.*
63 Ganis, G. (2009). The cognitive neuroscience of deception. *Social Neuroscience, 4*(6) 465–472.
64 A pioneering study in this regard is Langleben, D. (2008). Detection and Deception with fMRI: Are we there yet? *Legal and Criminological Psychology, 13*(1), 1–9.
65 Ganis, G. (2009). The cognitive neuroscience of deception. *Social Neuroscience, 4*(6), 465–472.
66 Barbara Sahakian interviewed by the author, May 2, 2023.
67 Altimus, C. M. (2017). Neuroscience has the power to change the criminal justice system. *Eneuro, 4*(1).
68 See: Pardo, M. S., & Patterson, D. (2013). *Minds, Brains, and Law: The Conceptual Foundations of Law and Neuroscience.* Oxford University Press.

69 American Psychological Association. (1974). Report of the task force on the role of psychology in the criminal justice system. *American Psychologist, 33,* 1099–1113, at 1110.
70 Based on: Archer, R. P., Buffington-Vollum, J. K., Stredny, R. V., & Handel, R. W. (2006). A survey of psychological test use patterns among forensic psychologists. *Journal of Personality Assessment, 87*(1), 84–94.
71 How India's neurocops used brainscans to convict murderers | WIRED.
72 How India's neurocops used brainscans to convict murderers | WIRED.
73 Nato, N. (2010). This brain test maps the truth.
74 The brain on trial: India's forensic mind-reading tool raises global eyebrows. The Researcher Daily.
75 *USA v Semrav, 2010 per Judge Pham.*
76 Coppola, F. (2018). Mapping the brain to predict antisocial behaviour: New frontiers in neurocriminology, 'new' challenges for criminal justice. *UCL Journal of Law and Jurisprudence-Special Issue, 1*(1), 103–126, p. 105.
77 Glenn, A. L., & Raine, A. (2014). Neurocriminology: Implications for the punishment, prediction and prevention of criminal behaviour. *Nature Reviews Neuroscience, 15*(1), 54-63, at 54.
78 Sahakian, B., & Gottwald, J. (2017). *Sex, Lies, and Brain Scans: How fMRI Reveals What Really Goes on in Our Minds*. Oxford University Press, p. 53.
79 Apps, Matthew A. J. (2016). Anterior cingulate gyrus and social cognition: Tracking the motivation of others. *Neuron, 90*(4), 692–707.
80 Hakun, J. G. (2008). fMRI investigation of the cognitive structure of concealed information test. *Neurocase, 14*(1), 59–67.
81 Nagel, T. (2023). *Moral Feelings, Moral Reality, and Moral Progress.* Oxford University Press, p. 2.
82 Nagel, *Moral Feelings*, p. 1.
83 Foot, P. (1967). The problem of abortion and the doctrine of the double effect. *Oxford Review, 5*(1), 5–15.
84 Gothard, T., & Davies, J. (2024). A spiking neuron model of moral judgment in trolley dilemmas. *Scientific Reports, 14*(1), p. 21733.
85 Gothard, T., & Davies, J. A spiking neuron model of moral judgment in trolley dilemma, 21734.
86 Deutsch, K. W. (1969). *Nationalism and its alternatives.* Alfred Knopf, p. 3.
87 Le Guin, U. *The left hand of darkness*, cited in L. Zmigrod. *The Ideological* Brain, cit op., p. 127.
88 https://www.theguardian.com/books/2017/mar/22/the-road-to-somewhere-david-goodhart-populist-revolt-future-politics
89 Abramowitz, A. I., & Webster, S. (2016). The rise of negative partisanship and the nationalization of US elections in the 21st century. *Electoral Studies, 41*, 12–22.
90 For some of these theories see: Pettigrew, T. F., Social psychological perspectives on Trump supporters. *Journal of Social and Political Psychology* 5, no. 1 (2017). https://doi.org/10.5964/jspp.v5i1.750
91 Phelps, E. A., O'Connor, K. J., Cunningham, W. A., Funayama, E. S., Gatenby, J. C., Gore, J. C., & Banaji, M. R. (2000). Performance on indirect measures of race evaluation predicts amygdala activation. *Journal of Cognitive Neuroscience, 12*(5), 729–738, p. 729.
92 Phelps, Performance on indirect measures of race evaluation predicts amygdala activation. ibid.
93 Phelps, Performance on indirect measures of race evaluation predicts amygdala activation. ibid.

94 Westen, D., Blagov, P. S., Harenski, K., Kilts, C., & Hamann, S. (2006). Neural bases of motivated reasoning: An fMRI study of emotional constraints on partisan political judgment in the 2004 US presidential election. *Journal of Cognitive Neuroscience, 18*(11), 1947–1958.
95 Hibbing, J. R. (2013). Ten misconceptions concerning neurobiology and politics. *Perspectives on Politics, 11*(2), 475–489, at p. 476.
96 Settle, J. et al. (2010). Friendships moderate an association between dopamine gene variant and political ideology. *Journal of Politics, 72*(4), 1189–1198, at p. 1189.
97 See especially: Jost, J. T., & Amodio, D. M. (2011). Political ideology as motivated social cognition: Behavioral and neuroscientific evidence. *Motivation and Emotion* 36(1), 65.
98 Bloom quoted in Jost, et al., Political ideology as motivated social cognition, p. 65.
99 Jost, et al. Political ideology as motivated social cognition, p. 65.
100 Xu, X., Zuo, X., Wang, X., & Han, S. (2009). Do you feel my pain? Racial group membership modulates empathic neural responses. *Journal of Neuroscience 29*(26), 8525–8529.
101 The research design was standard for similar studies. For the benefit of the uninitiated reader, it might be useful to cite the methodology as described by the researchers. It was carried out among 17 Chinese (8 males, mean 23 years, SD 2.0 years, all right-handed) and 16 Caucasian healthy college students (8 males, mean 23 years, SD 3.7 years, 10 Americans, 2 Dutch, 1 Italian, 1 German, 1 Russian, 1 Israeli, 12 right-handed, 4 left-handed) who were paid for participation. All had normal or corrected-to-normal vision and reported no abnormal neurological history. Informed consent was obtained from all participants before scanning. This study was approved by a local ethics committee. Stimuli and procedure: The stimuli consisted of 48 video clips showing faces of 6 Chinese (3 males) and 6 Caucasian models (3 males). Each clip, subtending a visual angle of 21° and 17° (width and height), at a viewing distance of 80 cm, lasted 3 s and depicted a face with neutral expressions receiving painful (needle penetration) or non-painful (Q-tip touch) stimulation applied to the left or right cheeks. After each video clip, participants were instructed to judge whether or not the model was [p. 8525] feeling pain by pressing a button using the right index or middle finger. Six functional scans of 204 s were obtained from each subject. Each scan consisted of 16 video clips (8 Chinese and 8 Caucasian faces, half with painful and half with non-painful stimulations in a random order). The interstimulus interval between two successive clips lasted 9 s during which participants fixated at a central cross. The last clip in each scan was followed by a fixation of 12 s. After the scanning procedure, participants were shown half of the video clips again and had to rate the pain intensity felt by the model ("How painful do you think the model feels?") and the unpleasantness felt by the onlooker ("How unpleasant do you feel when observing the video clip?") using a Likert-type scale where 0 indicated no effect and 10 indicated maximal effect (e.g., extremely painful, extremely unpleasant). Xu, "Do you feel my pain? Racial group membership modulates empathic neural responses", pp. 8525–8526.
102 Xu, X., Zuo, X., Wang, X., & Han, S. (2009). Do you feel my pain? Racial group membership modulates empathic neural responses. *Journal of Neuroscience, 29*(26), 8525–8529, at p. 8525
103 Cao, Y., Contreras-Huerta, L. S., McFadyen, J., & Cunnington, R. (2015). Racial bias in neural response to others' pain is reduced with other-race contact. *Cortex, 70*, 68–78.
104 Cao et al., *Racial Bias*, p. 68.
105 Descartes, R. (1987) [1637]. *Discours de la méthode*. Paris: Vrin, Part I, p. 10.
106 See: Bruneau, E., Jacoby, N., Kteily, N., & Axe, R. (2018). Denying humanity: The distinct neural correlates of blatant dehumanization. *Journal of Experimental Psychology: General, 147*(7), 1078–1093. Though it should be noted that Lasana Harris and colleagues conducted "a facial electromyography (fEMG) among a small set of participants, finding that revenge triggered significantly stronger negative emotions against outgroups than dehumanization". See: Kiper, J., Lillie,

C., Wilson, R. A., Knapp, B., Gwon, Y., & Harris, L. T. (2023). Dangerous speech: A cross-cultural study of dehumanization and revenge. *Journal of Cognition and Culture, 23*(1–2), 170–200, at p. 170.

107 https://www.reuters.com/world/americas/bolsonaro-eyes-dividend-tax-debt-pardon-brazil-campaign-turns-economy-2022-10-06/

108 https://www.washingtonpost.com/world/2022/10/31/bolsonaro-lula-brazil-election

109 Gurr, T. R. (1970) *Why Men Rebel?* Princeton University Press.

110 Gurr, *Why Men Rebel*, p. 257.

111 On unified Science see: Neurath, O. (2021). Unified science as encyclopedic integration. In M. Neurath, S. Sarkar, M. Schlick & R. Carnap. *Logical Empiricism at Its Peak: Schlick, Carnap, and Neurath* (pp. 309–335). Routledge. See further: O'Neill, J. (2003). Unified science as political philosophy: Positivism, pluralism and liberalism. *Studies in History and Philosophy of Science Part A, 34*(3), 575–596.

112 Following the defeat of then-president Jair Bolsonaro in the 2022 Brazilian general election and the inauguration of his successor, a mob of his supporters attacked Brazil's federal government buildings in the capital, Brasília. See: https://www.economist.com/the-americas/2023/01/12/a-copycat-insurrection-in-brazil-and-its-troubling-aftermath

113 Równiak, M., & Bogus-Nowakowska, K. (2020). The amygdala of the common shrew, guinea pig, rabbit, fox and pig: Five flavours of the mammalian amygdala as a consequence of clade-specific mosaic-like evolution. *Journal of Anatomy, 236*(5), 891–905.

114 For example, *Phaedo* 94b.

115 Plato *Republic*, IV. 440e.

116 Plato (1997). Phaedrus. In J. M. Cooper (Ed.), *Plato Complete Works* (pp. 506–556, p. 523 (245a)).

117 Plato. Phaedrus. *ibid.*

118 Dooley, R. (2015, November 20). Do neuromarketing and politics mix? *Forbes Magazine.*

119 Plato. (1997). In J. M. Cooper (Ed.), *Plato: Complete Works* (755). Hackett Publishing Company.

120 Cicero, Q. (2002). Handbook of electioneering. In D. R. Shackleton Bailey (Ed.), *Cicero: Letters to Quintus and Brutus, to Octavian, Invectives, Handbook of Electioneering* (p. 421). Harvard University Press.

121 Cummings, C. (2017, January). On the Referendum #22: Some Basic numbers for the Vote Leave Campaign.

122 Peston, R. (2018). *WTF*, p. 93. Hodder.

123 Kühn, S., Strelow, E., & Gallinat, J. (2016). Multiple "buy buttons" in the brain: Forecasting chocolate sales at point-of-sale based on functional brain activation using fMRI. *NeuroImage, 136*, 122–128.

124 Kühn, S., Strelow, E., & Gallinat, J. (2016). Multiple "buy buttons" in the brain: Forecasting chocolate sales at point-of-sale based on functional brain activation using fMRI. *NeuroImage, 136*, 122–128.

125 Corbit, L. H., & Balleine, B. W. (2016). Learning and motivational processes contributing to Pavlovian-instrumental transfer and their neural bases: Dopamine and beyond. *Current Topics in Behavioral Neurosciences, 27*, 259–89.

126 Nam, H. H., Jost, J. T., Meager, M. R., & Van Bavel, J. J. (2021). Toward a neuropsychology of political orientation: Exploring ideology in patients with frontal and midbrain lesions. *Philosophical Transactions of the Royal Society B, 376*(1822), 20200137.

127 Philiastides, M. G., Auksztulewicz, R., Heekeren, H. R., & Blankenburg, F. (2011). Causal role of dorsolateral prefrontal cortex in human perceptual decision making. *Current Biology, 21*(11), 980–983.
128 On economic decision making and the Dorsolateral Prefrontal Cortex, see e.g.: Yamagishi, T., Takagishi, H., Fermin, A. D. S. R., Kanai, R., Li, Y., & Matsumoto, Y. (2016). Cortical thickness of the dorsolateral prefrontal cortex predicts strategic choices in economic games. *Proceedings of the National Academy of Sciences, 113*(20), 5582–5587.
129 Nam, H. H., Jost, J. T., Meager, M. R., & Van Bavel, J. J. (2021). Toward a neuropsychology of political orientation: Exploring ideology in patients with frontal and midbrain lesions. *Philosophical Transactions of the Royal Society B, 376*(1822), 2.
130 Kato, J., Ide, H., Kabashima, I., Kadota, H., Takano, K., & Kansaku, K. (2009). Neural correlates of attitude change following positive and negative advertisements. *Frontiers in Behavioral Neuroscience, 6*, 1.
131 Goldstein, K., & Ridout, T. N. (2004). Measuring the effects of televised political advertising in the United States. *Annual Review of Political Science, 7*, 205–226.
132 *New York Times*, November 12, 2015. https://www.nytimes.com/2015/11/12/world/americas/mexicos-governing-party-vows-to-stop-using-neuromarketing-to-study-voters.html?_r=0
133 Wang, S., Yu, R., Tyszka, J. M., Zhen, S., Kovach, C., Sun, S., Huang, Y., Hurlemann, R., Ross, I. B., Chung, J. M., Mamelak, A. N., Adolphs, R., & Rutishauser, U. (2017). The human amygdala parametrically encodes the intensity of specific facial emotions and their categorical ambiguity. *Nature Communications, 8*, art. no. 14821.
134 Aquino, V. H. H. (2021, October 21). Neuropolítica, una nueva forma de ganar electioes. *Alcaldes Mexico*. https://www.alcaldesdemexico.com/notas-principales/neuropolitica-una-nueva-forma-de-ganar-elecciones/
135 Westen, D. (2008). The political brain: The role of emotion in deciding the fate of the nation. *Public Affairs*, 61–62.
136 Western, *The Political Brain*, p. 62.
137 This is famously argued by Karl R. Popper. For a brief overview see: Popper, K. R. (1963). Science as falsification. *Conjectures and Refutations 1*(1963), 33–39.
138 Jost, John T., and Amodio, D. M. Political ideology as motivated social cognition, p. 55.
139 Hochschild, A. R. (2018). *Strangers in Their Own Land: Anger and Mourning on the American Right*. The New Press.
140 Bechara, A., Damasio, H., and Damasio, A. R. (2000). Emotion, decision making and the orbitofrontal cortex. *Cerebral Cortex*, 10(3), 295–307.
141 Ahn, W. Y., Kishida, K. T., Gu, X., Lohrenz, T., Harvey, A., Alford, J. R., . . . & Montague, P. R. (2014). Nonpolitical images evoke neural predictors of political ideology. *Current Biology, 24*(22), 2693–2699.
142 Theodoridis, A. G., & Nelson, A. J. (2012). Of BOLD claims and excessive fears: A call for caution and patience regarding political neuroscience. *Political Psychology, 33*(1), 27–43, p. 27.
143 Zamboni, G., Gozzi, M., Krueger, F., Duhamel, J. R., Sirigu, A., & Grafman, J. (2009). Individualism, conservatism, and radicalism as criteria for processing political beliefs: A parametric fMRI study. *Social Neuroscience, 4*(5), 367–383, p. 367.
144 Fecteau, S., Pascual-Leone, A., Zald, D. H., Liguori, P., Théoret, H., Boggio, P. S., & Fregni, F. (2007). Activation of prefrontal cortex by transcranial direct current stimulation reduces appetite for risk during ambiguous decision making. *Journal of Neuroscience, 27*(23), 6212–6218.

145 Fliessbach, K., Weber, B., Trautner, P., Dohmen, T., Sunde, U., Elger, C. E., & Falk, A. (2007). Social comparison affects reward-related brain activity in the human ventral striatum. *Science, 318*(5854), 1305–1308.
146 The Love Actually and Mamma Mia star commissioned the research when he guest edited BBC Radio 4's Today programme in December 2022. During the program he asked scientists to scan the brains of politicians to see if there were any differences depending on political leanings. As a result of this, the researchers put him on the list of authors. So, it is perhaps slightly over-egging the pudding to call him a co-author though he is listed as such by the other authors of the paper. https://www.bbc.com/news/entertainment-arts-13661538
147 Kanai, R., Feilden, T., Firth, C., & Rees, G. (2011). Political orientations are correlated with brain structure in young adults. *Current Biology* 21(8), 677–680.
148 Lockwood, P. L., Apps, M. A., Roiser, J. P., & Viding, E. (2015). Encoding of vicarious reward prediction in anterior cingulate cortex and relationship with trait empathy. *Journal of Neuroscience, 35*(40), 13720–13727.
149 Morris, S. G. (2020). Empathy and the liberal-conservative political divide in the US. *Journal of Social and Political Psychology, 8*(1), 8–24.
150 Kanai, R., Feilden, T., Firth, C., & Rees, G. (2011). Political orientations are correlated with brain structure in young adults. *Current biology, 21*(8), 677–680.
151 Rule, N. O., Freeman, J. B., Moran, J. M., Gabrieli, J. D., Adams Jr, R. B., & Ambady, N. (2010). Voting behavior is reflected in amygdala response across cultures. *Social Cognitive and Affective Neuroscience, 5*(2–3), 349–355, p. 349.
152 Schreiber, D., Fonzo, G., Simmons, A. N., Dawes, C. T., Flagan, T., Fowler, J. H., & Paulus, M. P. (2013). Red brain, blue brain: Evaluative processes differ in Democrats and Republicans. *PLoS One, 8*(2), e52970.
153 Karpinski, A., & Hilton, J. L. (2001). Attitudes and the Implicit Association Test. *Journal of Personality and Social Psychology, 81*(5), 774–788.
154 Knutson, K. M., Wood, J. N., Spampinato, M. V., & Grafman, J. (2006). Politics on the brain: An fMRI investigation. *Social Neuroscience, 1*(1), 25–40, p. 25.
155 Sergent, J., Ohta, S., & MacDonald, B. (1992). Functional neuroanatomy of face and object processing. A positron emission tomography study. *Brain, 115*(1), 15–36.
156 Spezio, M. L., Rangel, A., Alvarez, R. M., O'Doherty, J. P., Mattes, K., Todorov, A., Kim, H., & Adolphs, R. A neural basis for the effect of candidate appearance on election outcomes. *Social Cognitive and Affective Neuroscience, 3*(4), 344–352.
157 Spezio. A neural basis for the effect of candidate appearance on election outcomes, p. 344.
158 Rigney, A. E., Koski, J. E., & Beer, J. S. (2018). The functional role of ventral anterior cingulate cortex in social evaluation: Disentangling valence from subjectively rewarding opportunities. *Social Cognitive and Affective Neuroscience, 13*(1), 14–21.
159 Gozzi, M., Zamboni, G., Krueger, F., & Grafman, J. (2010). Interest in politics modulates neural activity in the amygdala and ventral striatum. *Human Brain Mapping, 31*(11), 1763–1771.
160 Gozzi, Interest in politics modulates neural activity in the amygdala and ventral striatum, p. 1763.
161 Gozzi, Interest in politics modulates neural activity in the amygdala and ventral striatum, p. 1763.
162 Viñas-Guasch, N., & Wu, Y. J. (2017). The role of the putamen in language: A meta-analytic connectivity modeling study. *Brain Structure and Function, 222*, 3991–4004.

163 Hong, S.-B., Harrison, B. J., Dandash, O., Choi, E.-J., Kim, S.-C., Kim, H.-H., Shim, D.-H., Kim, C.-D., Kim, J.-W., & Yi, S.-H. A selective involvement of putamen functional connectivity in youth with internet gaming disorder. *Brain Research* 1602 (2015), 85–95.
164 Almond, G. A., & Verba, S. (2015). *The Civic Culture: Political Attitudes and Democracy in Five Nations.* Princeton University Press.
165 Sapolsky, R. (2019). This is your brain on nationalism: The Biology of Us and them. *Foreign Affairs*, 98(2), 42–47, at p. 42.
166 Thucydides. (1954). *The Peloponnesian War.* Penguin Books.
167 Penfield, W. (1938). The cerebral cortex in man: I. The cerebral cortex and consciousness. *Archives of Neurology & Psychiatry, 40*(3), 417–442.
168 Ryle, G. [1949] 2002. *The Concept of Mind*, p. 11. The University of Chicago Press.
169 Wilson, E. O. (1975). *Sociobiology: The New Synthesis.* Harvard University Press.
170 Wilson, *Sociobiology*, p. x.
171 Buhs, J. B. (2004). *The Fire Ant Wars: Nature, Science, and Public Policy in Twentieth-Century America*, pp. 32–34. University of Chicago Press.
172 Kant, I. (2011). *Observations on the Feeling of the Beautiful and Sublime*, ed. P. Frierson & P. Guyer, p. 58 (AA II, 253). Cambridge University Press.
173 Kant, I. (1968) [1788]. Über den Gebrauch teleologischer Principien in der Philosophie. Werkausgabe in 12 BändenIX: Schriften zur Naturphilosophie. Frankfurt aM: Suhrkamp Verlag, p. 176.
174 Reuters. (2024, October 10). Religious hate crimes up 25% in England and Wales, driven by anti-Jewish offences.
175 Greenwald, A. G., McGhee, D. E., & Schwartz, J. K. L. (1998). Measuring individual differences in implicit cognition: The Implicit Association Test. *Journal of Personality and Social Psychology, 74*(6), 1464–1480.
176 Feinstein, J. S., Adolphs, R., Damasio, A., & Tranel, D. (2011). The human amygdala and the induction and experience of fear. *Current biology, 21*(1), 34–38, p. 34.
177 Wicker, B., Keysers, C., Plailly, J., Royet, J. P., Gallese, V., & Rizzolatti, G. (2003). Both of us disgusted in My insula: The common neural basis of seeing and feeling disgust. *Neuron, 40*(3), 655–664.
178 Stevens, F. L., Hurley, R. A., & Taber, K. H. (2011). Anterior cingulate cortex: Unique role in cognition and emotion. *The Journal of Neuropsychiatry and Clinical Neurosciences, 23*(2), 121–125.
179 Terbeck, S., Kahane, G., McTavish, S., Savulescu, J., Cowen, P. J., & Hewstone, M. (2012). Propranolol reduces implicit negative racial bias. *Psychopharmacology, 222*, 419–424.
180 Bertrand, M., & Mullainathan, S. (2004). Are Emily and Greg more employable than Lakisha and Jamal? A field experiment on labor market discrimination. *American Economic Review, 94*(4), 991–1013.
181 Noar, S. M. (2006). A 10 year retrospective of research in health mass media campaigns: Where do we go from here? *Journal of Public Health Communication, 11*(1), 21–42.
182 Falk, E. B., Berkman, E. T., Whalen, D., & Lieberman, M. D. (2011). Neural activity during health messaging predicts reductions in smoking above and beyond self-report. *Health Psychology, 30*(2), 177.
183 Falk, E. B., Berkman, E. T., & Lieberman, M. D. (2012). From neural responses to population behavior: Neural focus group predicts population-level media effects. *Psychological Science, 23*(5), 439–445.
184 Sahakian, B. J., & Gottwald, J. (2017). *Sex, Lies, and Brain Scans: How fMRI Reveals What Really Goes on in Our Minds*, p. 105. Oxford University Press.

185 Falk, E. B., O'Donnell, M. B., Tompson, S., Gonzalez, R., Dal Cin, S., Strecher, V., . . . & An, L. (2016). Functional brain imaging predicts public health campaign success. *Social Cognitive and Affective Neuroscience, 11*(2), 204–214.
186 Langleben, D. D., Loughead, J. W., Ruparel, K., Hakun, J. G., Busch-Winokur, S., Holloway, M. B., Strasser, A. A., Cappella, J. N., & Lerman, C. (2009). Reduced prefrontal and temporal processing and recall of high "sensation value" ads. *Neuroimage, 46*(1), 219–225.
187 Falk, E. B., Brook O'Donnell, M., Tompson, S., Gonzalez, R., Dal Cin, S., Strecher, V., Cummings, K. M., & An, L. (2016). Functional brain imaging predicts public health campaign success. *Social Cognitive and Affective Neuroscience, 11*(2), 204–214.
188 Gen Z: Less than half of 16-24-year-olds watch traditional TV, Ofcom says – BBC News.
189 Instagram Video Statistics 2025 ± IGTV Stats (Latest Data) – EarthWeb.
190 Šola, H. M., Qureshi, F. H., & Khawaja, S. (2024). Exploring the untapped potential of neuromarketing in online learning: Implications and challenges for the higher education sector in Europe. *Behavioral Sciences, 14*(2), 80.
191 Lazarsfeld, P. F., Berelson, B., & Gaudet, H. (1968). *The People's Choice: How the Voter Makes Up His Mind in a Presidential Campaign.* Columbia University Press.
192 Ercegovac, I., Tankosic, M., & Grilec, A. (2022). Influence of two-step flow theory supported by neuromarketing methods on consumers perception – The theoretical overview. *Economic and Social Development: Book of Proceedings*, 91–102.
193 Lazarsfeld, P. F., Berelson, B. R., & Gaudet, H. Erie County Study, 1940. [distributor], 2006-01-12. https://doi.org/10.3886/ICPSR07204.v1.
194 Elihu K., & Lazarsfeld, P. F. (1955). *Personal Influence*, p. 309. Free Press.
195 See e.g.: Bennett, W. L., & Manheim, J. B. (November 2006). The one-step flow of communication. *The Annals of the American Academy of Political and Social Science, 608*(1), 213–232.
196 Choi, S. (December 2015). The two-step flow of communication in Twitter-based public forums. *Social Science Computer Review, 33*(6), 696–711.
197 Hilbert, M., Vásquez, J., Halpern, D., Valenzuela, S., & Arriagada, E. (August 2017). One step, two step, network step? Complementary perspectives on communication flows in twittered citizen protests. *Social Science Computer Review, 35*(4), 444–461, p. 444.
198 UK Government Foresight Project Report SR-E1, p. 2, quoted in S.-J. Blakemore (2015). The social brain in adolescence and the potential impact of social neuroscience on education. In J. Decety & J. T. Cacioppo (Eds.), *The Oxford Handbook of Social Neuroscience* (pp. 992–1000, 992). Oxford University Press.
199 Yu, L. (2022). *Vulnerable Minds: The Neuropolitics of Divided Societies.* Columbia University Press, p. XVIII.
200 Schmitt, C. (2015) [1932]. *Der Begriff des Politischen.* Duncker & Humblot, p. 25. Author's translation.
201 Lincoln, A. *Gettysburg Address*, November 19, 1863.
202 Madison, J. (2003). Federalist Paper No. 10. In A. Hamilton, J. Madison & J. Jay, *The Federalist Papers (1963)* (p. 72). Signet Books.
203 Andrews, *Neuropsychology*, p. 8.
204 Coolidge, F. L., Wynn, T., Overmann, K. A., & Hicks, J. M. (2014). Cognitive archaeology and the cognitive sciences. In E. Bruner (Ed.), *Human Paleoneurology* (pp. 177–208). Springer International Publishing.
205 Gannon, P. J., Holloway, R. L., Broadfield, D. C., & Braun, A. R. (1998). Asymmetry of chimpanzee planum temporale: Humanlike pattern of Wernicke's brain language area homolog. *Science, 279*(5348), 220–222.

206 Biden calls out governors who dropped mask rule for 'Neanderthal thinking'. Accessed June 10, 2025.
207 Lewin, R. (1993). *The Origin of Modern Humans.* American Scientific Library, p. 25.
208 Andrews, D. (2016). *Neuropsychology.* Routledge, p. 4.
209 Tattersall, J. (2009). Language and the origin of symbolic thought. In S. A. Beaune et al. (Eds.), *Cognitive Archaeology and Human Evolution* (pp. 109–117, p. 113). Cambridge University Press.
210 Barber, B. (1984). *Strong Democracy: Participatory Politics for a New Age.* University of California Press.
211 Arendt, H. (1959) *The Human Condition.* Doubleday.
212 Aristotle. *Nicomachean Ethics*, III, iii, 11.
213 Aristotle. *Nicomachean Ethics*, III, iii, 12.
214 Masaryk, T. G., & Capek, K. (1944). *Masaryk on Thought and Life. Conversations with Karel Capek.* Translated from the Czech by M. & R. Weatherall (p. 191). George Allen & Unwin Ltd.
215 For a discussion of the more recent theories of philosophy pertaining to the brain, see: Hohwy, J. (2016). The self-evidencing brain. *Noûs, 50*(2), 259–285.
216 Hippocrates of Cos. (1926). *The Sacred Disease.* Loeb, 174.
217 On this fascinating topic see: Ehrman, B. D. (2021). *Heaven and Hell: A History of the Afterlife.* Simon and Schuster.
218 Plato. (1892). *The Republic.* Macmillan, p. 299.
219 See: René Descartes, *Meditationes de Prima Philosophia, II.8.*
220 Spinoza. *Ethics*, Part III, Proposition 2.
221 Locke, J. (1689). *An Essay Concerning Human Understanding.* Book IV, Chapter III, 6.
222 Ryle,' G. (1949). *The Concept of Mind*, p. 13. University of Chicago Press.
223 Quantum mechanics and the consciousness connection. American Association for the Advancement of Science (AAAS).
224 Plassmann, H., Ramsøy, T. Z., & Milosavljevic, M. (2012). Branding the brain: A critical review and outlook. *Journal of Consumer Psychology, 22*(1), 18–36.
225 Douglas R Oxley, D. R., Smith, K. B., Alford, J. R., Hibbing, M. V., Miller, J. L., Scalora, M., Hatemi, P. K., & Hibbing, J. R. (2008). Political attitudes vary with physiological traits. *Science, 321*, 1667–1670, p. 1667.
226 Modell, A. H. (2012). Psychoanalysis, neuroscience, and the unconscious self. *The Psychoanalytic Review, 99*(4), 475–483.
227 Salzinger, K. (1973). Inside the black box, with apologies to Pandora: A review of Ulric Neisser's cognitive psychology. *Journal of the Experimental Analysis of Behavior, 19*(2), 369–378.
228 Without bragging, I predicted the outcome of the Brexit referendum four months before the vote in a peer-reviewed article using these "econometric" (or "politometric" models). See: Qvortrup, M. (2016). Referendums on Membership and European Integration 1972–2015. *The Political Quarterly, 87*(1), 61–70.
229 Evidently, I must have done something right, for I was awarded the Prize of the Best Article at the Political Studies Association in 2012 for my article Terrorism and political science: Qvortrup, M. (2012). Terrorism and political science. *The British Journal of Politics and International Relations, 14*(4), 503–517.
230 Bogaards, M. (2020). Coding, concessions, conclusions: A reply to Matt Qvortrup. *Studies in Conflict & Terrorism, 43*(10), 910–912, 910 and 912.
231 Plato, The *Republic* IV, 439e.
232 Schreiber, D. (2017). Neuropolitics: Twenty years later. *Politics and the Life Sciences, 36*(2), 114–131.

233 Hume, D. (1896). *A Treatise of Human Nature*. Clarendon Press, p. 1.
234 Magrini, M. (2021) *The Brain: A User's Manual.* Octopus Books, p. 138.
235 Haas, I. J., Warren, C., & Lauf, S. J. (2020). Political neuroscience: Understanding how the brain makes political decisions. In *Oxford Research Encyclopedia of Politics*.
236 Nozick, R. (1973). *Anarchy, State and Utopia.* Blackwell, p. xii.
237 See e.g.: Sperry, R. W., Zaidel, E., & Zaidel, D. (1979). Self-recognition and social awareness in the deconnected minor hemisphere. *Neuropsychologia, 17*(2), 153–166.
238 See: Bandettini, P. A. (2012). Functional MRI: A confluence of fortunate circumstances. *Neuroimage, 61*(2), A3–A11).
239 See: Belcher, A., & Sinnott-Armstrong, W. (2010). Neurolaw. *Wiley Interdisciplinary Reviews: Cognitive Science, 1*(1), 18–22.
240 Denworth, L. (2020, October 26). Conservative and liberal brains might have some real differences: Scanners try to watch the red-blue divide play out underneath the skull. *Scientific American.*
241 Andrews, D. (2016). *Neuropsychology.* Routledge, p. 7.
242 Shakespeare, S. *Macbeth*, V.iii, 44.

www.ingramcontent.com/pod-product-compliance
Lightning Source LLC
LaVergne TN
LVHW052157220926
848675LV00027B/298